The publisher and the University of California Press Foundation gratefully acknowledge the generous support of the Joan Palevsky Endowment Fund in Literature in Translation.

The Life of the Syrian Saint Barsauma

TRANSFORMATION OF THE CLASSICAL HERITAGE

Peter Brown, General Editor

I. *Art and Ceremony in Late Antiquity*, by Sabine G. MacCormack

II. *Synesius of Cyrene: Philosopher-Bishop*, by Jay Alan Bregman

III. *Theodosian Empresses: Women and Imperial Dominion in Late Antiquity*, by Kenneth G. Holum

IV. *John Chrysostom and the Jews: Rhetoric and Reality in the Late Fourth Century*, by Robert L. Wilken

V. *Biography in Late Antiquity: The Quest for the Holy Man*, by Patricia Cox

VI. *Pachomius: The Making of a Community in Fourth-Century Egypt*, by Philip Rousseau

VII. *Change in Byzantine Culture in the Eleventh and Twelfth Centuries*, by A. P. Kazhdan and Ann Wharton Epstein

VIII. *Leadership and Community in Late Antique Gaul*, by Raymond Van Dam

IX. *Homer the Theologian: Neoplatonist Allegorical Reading and the Growth of the Epic Tradition*, by Robert Lamberton

X. *Procopius and the Sixth Century*, by Averil Cameron

XI. *Guardians of Language: The Grammarian and Society in Late Antiquity*, by Robert A. Kaster

XII. *Civic Coins and Civic Politics in the Roman East, A.D. 180–275*, by Kenneth Harl

XIII. *Holy Women of the Syrian Orient*, introduced and translated by Sebastian P. Brock and Susan Ashbrook Harvey

XIV. *Gregory the Great: Perfection in Imperfection*, by Carole Straw

XV. *"Apex Omnium": Religion in the "Res gestae" of Ammianus*, by R. L. Rike

XVI. *Dioscorus of Aphrodito: His Work and His World*, by Leslie S. B. MacCoull

XVII. *On Roman Time: The Codex-Calendar of 354 and the Rhythms of Urban Life in Late Antiquity*, by Michele Renee Salzman

XVIII. *Asceticism and Society in Crisis: John of Ephesus and "The Lives of the Eastern Saints,"* by Susan Ashbrook Harvey

XIX. *Barbarians and Politics at the Court of Arcadius*, by Alan Cameron and Jacqueline Long, with a contribution by Lee Sherry

XX. *Basil of Caesarea*, by Philip Rousseau

XXI. *In Praise of Later Roman Emperors: The Panegyrici Latini*, introduction, translation, and historical commentary by C. E. V. Nixon and Barbara Saylor Rodgers

XXII. *Ambrose of Milan: Church and Court in a Christian Capital*, by Neil B. McLynn

XXIII. *Public Disputation, Power, and Social Order in Late Antiquity*, by Richard Lim

XXIV. *The Making of a Heretic: Gender, Authority, and the Priscillianist Controversy*, by Virginia Burrus

XXV. *Symeon the Holy Fool: Leontius's "Life" and the Late Antique City*, by Derek Krueger

XXVI. *The Shadows of Poetry: Vergil in the Mind of Augustine*, by Sabine MacCormack

XXVII. *Paulinus of Nola: Life, Letters, and Poems*, by Dennis E. Trout

XXVIII. *The Barbarian Plain: Saint Sergius between Rome and Iran*, by Elizabeth Key Fowden

XXIX. *The Private Orations of Themistius*, translated, annotated, and introduced by Robert J. Penella

XXX. *The Memory of the Eyes: Pilgrims to Living Saints in Christian Late Antiquity*, by Georgia Frank

XXXI. *Greek Biography and Panegyric in Late Antiquity*, edited by Tomas Hägg and Philip Rousseau

XXXII. *Subtle Bodies: Representing Angels in Byzantium*, by Glenn Peers

XXXIII. *Wandering, Begging Monks: Spiritual Authority and the Promotion of Monasticism in Late Antiquity*, by Daniel Caner

XXXIV. *Failure of Empire: Valens and the Roman State in the Fourth Century* A.D., by Noel Lenski

XXXV. *Merovingian Mortuary Archaeology and the Making of the Early Middle Ages*, by Bonnie Effros

XXXVI. *Quṣayr 'Amra: Art and the Umayyad Elite in Late Antique Syria*, by Garth Fowden

XXXVII. *Holy Bishops in Late Antiquity: The Nature of Christian Leadership in an Age of Transition*, by Claudia Rapp

XXXVIII. *Encountering the Sacred: The Debate on Christian Pilgrimage in Late Antiquity*, by Brouria Bitton-Ashkelony

XXXIX. *There Is No Crime for Those Who Have Christ: Religious Violence in the Christian Roman Empire*, by Michael Gaddis

XL. *The Legend of Mar Qardagh: Narrative and Christian Heroism in Late Antique Iraq*, by Joel Thomas Walker

XLI. *City and School in Late Antique Athens and Alexandria*, by Edward J. Watts

XLII. *Scenting Salvation: Ancient Christianity and the Olfactory Imagination*, by Susan Ashbrook Harvey

XLIII. *Man and the Word: The Orations of* Himerius, edited by Robert J. Penella

XLIV. *The Matter of the Gods*, by Clifford Ando

XLV. *The Two Eyes of the Earth: Art and Ritual of Kingship between Rome and Sasanian Iran*, by Matthew P. Canepa

XLVI. *Riot in Alexandria: Tradition and Group Dynamics in Late Antique Pagan and Christian Communities*, by Edward J. Watts

XLVII. *Peasant and Empire in Christian North Africa*, by Leslie Dossey

XLVIII. *Theodoret's People: Social Networks and Religious Conflict in Late Roman Syria*, by Adam M. Schor

XLIX. *Sons of Hellenism, Fathers of the Church: Emperor Julian, Gregory of Nazianzus, and the Vision of Rome*, by Susanna Elm

L. *Shenoute of Atripe and the Uses of Poverty: Rural Patronage, Religious Conflict, and Monasticism in Late Antique Egypt*, by Ariel G. López

LI. *Doctrine and Power: Theological Controversy and Christian Leadership in the Later Roman Empire*, by Carlos R. Galvão-Sobrinho

LII. *Crisis of Empire: Doctrine and Dissent at the End of Late Antiquity*, by Phil Booth

LIII. *The Final Pagan Generation*, by Edward J. Watts

LIV. *The Mirage of the Saracen: Christians and Nomads in the Sinai Peninsula in Late Antiquity*, by Walter D. Ward

LV. *Missionary Stories and the Formation of the Syriac Churches*, by Jeanne-Nicole Mellon Saint-Laurent

LVI. *A State of Mixture: Christians, Zoroastrians, and Iranian Political Culture in Late Antiquity*, by Richard E. Payne

LVII. *Constantine and the Captive Christians of Persia: Martyrdom and Religious Identity in Late Antiquity*, by Kyle Smith

LVIII. *In the Image of Origen: Eros, Virtue, and Constraint in the Early Christian Academy*, by David Satran

LVIX. *Being Christian in Vandal Africa: The Politics of Orthodoxy in the Post-Imperial West*, by Robin Whelan

LX. *The Wandering Holy Man: The Life of Barsauma, Christian Asceticism, and Religious Conflict in Late Antique Palestine*, edited by Johannes Hahn and Volker Menze

LXI. *The Life of the Syrian Saint Barsauma: Eulogy of a Hero of the Resistance to the Council of Chalcedon*, translated by Andrew N. Palmer

LX. *The Wandering Holy Man: The Life of Barsauma, Christian Asceticism, and Religious Conflict in Late Antique Palestine*, edited by Johannes Hahn and Volker Menze

LXI. *The Life of the Syrian Saint Barsauma: Eulogy of a Hero of the Resistance to the Council of Chalcedon*, translated by Andrew N. Palmer

The Life of the Syrian Saint Barsauma

Eulogy of a Hero of the Resistance to the Council of Chalcedon

Translated by Andrew N. Palmer

UNIVERSITY OF CALIFORNIA PRESS

University of California Press
Oakland, California

Library of Congress Cataloging-in-Publication Data

Names: Palmer, Andrew N., translator.
Title: The life of the Syrian Saint Barsauma : eulogy of a hero of the resistance to the Council of Chalcedon / Andrew N. Palmer.
Other titles: Barṣawmā. English
Description: Oakland, California : University of California Press, [2020] | Series: Transformation of the Classical Heritage; 61
Identifiers: LCCN 2020001694 (print) | LCCN 2020001695 (ebook) | ISBN 9780520304161 (cloth) | ISBN 9780520304178 (paperback) | ISBN 9780520972988 (ebook)
Subjects: LCSH: Barṣawmā, Saint, –456. | Syriac Christian saints—Biography.
Classification: LCC BX179.B385 A3 2020 (print) | LCC BX179.B385 (ebook) | DDC 270.2092 [B]—dc23
LC record available at https://lccn.loc.gov/2020001694
LC ebook record available at https://lccn.loc.gov/202000169

Manufactured in the United States of America

25 24 23 22 21 20 19 18
10 9 8 7 6 5 4 3 2 1

This translation is dedicated to the memory of Gevrey Kodaş

CONTENTS

Introduction

"Scelestissimus pseudomonachus." That is how Barsauma, a fifth-century Syrian, is described in the *Bibliotheca Orientalis*, the eighteenth-century encyclopedia compiled by J. S. Assemanus, for many years the chief authority on the Syrian churches.[1] "A hardened criminal, masquerading as a monk": seven words are needed to render into English the superlative epithet and disdainful compound of the Latin. The crime of which Barsauma was accused was murder—and not just any murder: Saint Flavian, the man he is said to have killed, was the bishop of the greatest city of Christendom and so, in a certain sense, the highest-ranking patriarch of the civilized world. The source from which Assemanus distilled his annihilating description—the Acts of the Council of Chalcedon, held in the year 451—carried the combined authority of the Catholic Church and the Roman Empire.[2]

Assemanus, a Lebanese Catholic, was selective in his acquisition of Syriac codices, notably rejecting a venerable manuscript that was shown to him in a Coptic monastery. More than a hundred years later this great codex, made under the supervision of Michael the Great, patriarch of the Syrian Orthodox Church from 1166 to 1199, was sold to the British

1. J. S. Assemanus, *Bibliotheca Orientalis Clementino-Vaticana*, vols. 1, 2, 3.1, 3.2 (Rome, 1719–28); vol. 2 (Rome, 1721), Caput I, p. 9: "scelestissimi pseudomonachi."

2. A. Palmer, "The West-Syrian Monastic Founder Barṣawmo: A Historical Review of the Scholarly Literature," in *Orientalia Christiana: Festschrift für Hubert Kaufhold*, ed. P. Bruns and H. O. Luthe (Wiesbaden: Harrassowitz, 2013), 399–413.

nation.[3] This book once contained the *Lives* of about eighty holy men. When complete, it held five hundred leaves, but many of these are now lost, including the whole of the first gathering: five great sheets of parchment, folded like a newspaper to make twenty pages, a quinion. Pride of place on these folios had been given to Barsauma, the beginning of whose *Life* therefore had to be pieced together from two other incomplete manuscripts, until a complete copy was found in the Patriarchal Library of the Syrian Orthodox Church. Damascus MS 12/17, the volume in which this copy of the *Life* is included, is the first part of another originally massive codex prepared ten years earlier under the supervision of the same Patriarch Michael. It is this copy that is translated here.[4]

Barsauma is a hero to the Oriental Orthodox Churches, a villain to the Greek Orthodox and the Roman Catholics. The *Life* sings his praises, the Acts of Chalcedon deny that he deserves them. Evidently both parties exaggerate; the historical Barsauma was certainly not free from *odium theologicum*, the besetting vice of all fundamentalists: the hatred of those who call their truth into question. But is there enough evidence to convict him of religious terrorism? According to his own supporters, he destroyed places of worship belonging to other religions. But this, to the Church of the Christian empire in the fifth century, was justified by the example of Josiah and others.[5] The irony is that Josiah revived the monotheistic religion of his kingdom, Judah, and suppressed paganism, whereas the Christians wanted to use his precedent to make Judaism itself obsolete.

Anti-Semitism was rife, and the political will to stem it was lacking. Roman law protected the Jews against vandalism and assault and provided for compensation. But Barsauma and his fellow zealots were never convicted, though some of them were present when a large number of Jews, lamenting the ruins of their Temple at Jerusalem, were killed, allegedly by angels! There must be some truth in the report of their brief imprisonment, since the *Life* says, defensively, that

3. British Library, Add. MS 12,174, made at the monastery of Saint Barsauma in the year 1196.

4. Recently, the Hill Museum & Manuscript Library has published images of further copies of this text; but Damascus 12/17 remains the best single witness.

5. The life of Josiah is narrated in the Hebrew Bible (2 Kings 22–23; 2 Chronicles 34–35).

Barsauma was not himself among those arrested. It is not improbable that the civil authorities, who were also Christians, were deterred by an impressive holy man from prosecuting men who had assaulted the Jews—though the *Life* denies this.

In the year 388 Theodosius I had decreed that the bishop of Callinicum should rebuild the synagogue burned down at his instigation. Saint Ambrose had challenged this from the pulpit in Milan, making the emperor revoke his decree and do penance for befriending the enemies of Christ. Assemanus's condemnation of Barsauma rests, not on any assault the zealot may have made on the Jews, but on his alleged murder of a Christian prelate. After weighing all the evidence Henry Chadwick concluded, in 1955, that Flavian survived any injuries he may have sustained at Ephesus in the year 449, when Barsauma was present. Indeed, there is no contemporary proof that Flavian was attacked there. Most probably, Chadwick concludes, Pulcheria intentionally caused his death by instructing that he should be made to undertake an arduous winter journey on foot in bad health. The accusation was brought against Barsauma in order to deflect attention from this imperially sanctioned crime.[6]

The crucial evidence exonerating the Syrian monk is provided by his enemy, Nestorius. The writer of the *Life* did not know that there were such excellent grounds for his hero's acquittal, which he attributed to God's direct intervention; and Barsauma's judge may indeed have fallen ill and died. François Nau, who published a summary of the contents of the *Life*, certainly knew—and suppressed—the crucial evidence for the defense, which had been published earlier by the same François Nau.[7] Nau was no impartial judge, but a Catholic propagandist. By condemning Barsauma, Assemanus, another Catholic priest, had meant to discredit those "so-called Orthodox Churches" that regarded him as a saint.[8] Nau now blinkered his own erudition

6. H. Chadwick, "The Exile and Death of Flavian of Constantinople," *Journal of Theological Studies*, n.s., 6.1 (1955): 17–34.

7. Nestorius, *Le livre d'Héraclide de Damas*, trans. F. Nau (Paris: Letouzey et Ané, 1910). For Nau's summary of the *Life*, with which historians have had to be content until now, see his "Résumé," cited below in note 9.

8. The words "le chiese cosidette ortodosse" were used by the current bishop of Rome in an epistle read out at a conference held at the Pontificio Istituto Orientale on 26 October 2018 on the occasion of the opening of the academic year.

and harnessed its power to Assemanus's, as a second horse to draw the wagon of this agenda. By the early twentieth century, the scholarly public had become more diverse. In journals read by Orientalists, many of whom were Jews themselves, Nau could make Barsauma's name even more odious by drawing attention to his anti-Semitism. He must have intended the words "a Zionist movement" (from the title of one of his works) as a contemporary allusion.[9]

Having established that the accusation made against Barsauma at the Council of Chalcedon was unfounded, can we expect the source translated here to explain how this man came to be so important for the churches which find that council an obstacle to the unification of all Christians? The *Life* of Barsauma, who died in 456, is a rhetorical text, more like a funeral speech than a biography. As in the case of the earliest *Life* of Symeon, who died in 459, the writer appears to have been a disciple of the saint, and his audience, the pilgrims—simple countryfolk for the most part—who continued to flock to his monastery after his death. Ascetics such as Symeon, who stood for over thirty years on top of a pillar, and Barsauma, who never lay or even sat down for over fifty years, were called "athletes" by their panegyrists. There is a pronounced element of competition in the claims that were made for them, and the saints themselves seem to have lived with a view to winning a prize. Symeon is said to have dreamed that an angel promised him universal fame. But they evidently played a role in society, usually defending the poor against their oppressors. Barsauma takes a stance against the signatories to Chalcedon and treats these bishops, too, as oppressors of the peasantry.[10] Symeon, on the other hand, is claimed by Chalcedonians and non-Chalcedonians alike. The key to Barsauma's popularity in the non-Chalcedonian churches is precisely that his

9. F. Nau, "Barsauma," *Dictionnaire de théologie catholique* (Paris: Letouzey et Ané, 1905), 2:434–35; Nau, "Résumé de monographies syriaques," *Revue de l'Orient chrétien* 18 (1913): 270–76 and 379–89; 19 (1914): 113–34 and 278–89 (summary of the *Life of Barsauma* with select extracts in Syriac and French); Nau, "Deux épisodes de l'histoire juive sous Théodose II (423 et 438) d'après la Vie de Barsauma le Syrien," *Revue des études juives* 93 (1927): 184–206; Nau, "Sur la synagogue de Rabbat Moab (422) et un mouvement sioniste favorisé par l'impératrice Eudocie (438) d'après la Vie de Barsauma le Syrien," *Journal asiatique* 210 (1927): 189–92.

10. See A. Palmer, "A Tale of Two Synods: The Archimandrite Barsumas at Ephesus in 449 and at Chalcedon in 451," *Journal of Eastern Christian Studies* 66 (2014): 37–61.

theological position, unlike that of Symeon, was clearly against Chalcedon.

The *Life of Symeon* survives in a fifth-century manuscript, which already attributes many miracles to the intercession of the holy man.[11] Over the centuries, even more wonderful stories were added to the *Life of Barsauma*. The tabular overview at the end of this introduction suggests one mechanism by which the text had grown before its final redaction: each chapter began on a new page, and so there was a blank space at the bottom of the last pages of chapters 1, 4, 6, 8 and 10, where new miracles were added. Margins were left around the text, and here, too, short stories could be added, which later copyists supposed had been omitted by accident, like a word one finds in the margin of a letter. In good faith, these scribes included them in the body of the text. The text may also have been inflated by scribes who included miracles that until then had been told by word of mouth, not written down. To prove this, one would have to analyze their style and show that it differs from that of the original author.

The important conclusion from this is that passages taken from a miracle story that may or may not have been added later cannot be used to date the original text, or to contest its orthodoxy. It can be argued on internal evidence that the *Life of Barsauma* was written in 456/7, immediately after the death of its hero, perhaps as a eulogy to be pronounced on the anniversary of that event. Theodoret of Cyrrhus died in the early 460s, so § 151 must be later than that. Symeon the Stylite had died already in 459, but the encounter in § 46 (anticipated in §§ 32–33.) seems to draw on a written source and so must have been added later still. In § 137 a demon, claiming to speak the truth under compulsion, speaks through a possessed woman: "If the body of Jesus is like a human body, which human being has broken his body and given it as food to his friends? And if the blood of the Crucified, the Firstborn, is like the blood of the human race, what human blood can atone for sin?" Around the year 520 Julian of Halicarnassus began to teach that the body of Christ was not like a human body. This miracle story may therefore have been added to the *Life* after that

11. This codex, dated to the year 474, can be read (from right to left) by clicking on the icon of an open book at www.mss.vatlib.it/guii/scan/link.jsp > Vat.sir. > Vat.sir. 160. The earliest copies of the *Life of Barsauma* must have looked very much like this codex.

year by a crypto-Julianist, who guarded himself by putting the controversial doctrine in the mouth of a woman—and having her speak under the influence of the demon that possessed her. Demons in the Gospel of Mark speak the truth about Jesus, so Julianists could still use this passage as a proof-text, as Barhebraeus (who thought—anachronistically—that the Julianist author was Barsauma's disciple) said they did.

It is time to give a brief summary of the *Life*, followed by a detailed breakdown in tabular form. Barsauma came from the district of Samosata on the river Euphrates. His father died soon after his birth, and his mother remarried. The small boy ran away from his stepfather and, claiming to be an orphan, attached himself to a vagrant ascetic called Abraham. When Abraham died, he made a barefoot pilgrimage to Jerusalem alone. On returning, he settled in a cave near the village where he was born. One night, when he lay down to rest under the stars, it struck him that he, a servant, must forever stand in the presence of his master, God.

Barsauma was joined by like-minded men who became his disciples. In the spring they followed the flocks up to the high mountain pastures. Perhaps they drank the milk of the sheep and goats. Certainly they grazed on roots, in the summer they picked mulberries near the Euphrates, in the autumn they ate wild grapes. In the winter Barsauma endured the snow and ice, standing outside to chant his prayers, while his disciples sang their responses from their cave-monastery. Soon miracles, especially of exorcism, began to be attributed to the presence of the holy man, who had cut out more from his diet than seems possible for a mere human.

With forty disciples Barsauma made a second pilgrimage to Jerusalem. On their way they demolished pagan temples and the synagogues of Jews and Samaritans. Symeon the Stylite told his followers what a great ascetic Barsauma was, and the two saints met and blessed one another. After Barsauma's return, further miracles occurred in the region of Claudias, where his monastery was situated: bad water became fit to drink, barren fields produced a harvest, an infertile woman gave birth. Barsauma's curse, too, was effective: vines ceased to bear fruit, rich men and administrators died, the plague broke out. But Barsauma could put a stop to an epidemic by his prayers. Followers of Barsauma claimed to have seen him humbling Satan and being comforted by one of the seraphim.

With a hundred disciples Barsauma made a third visit to Jerusalem. The effects of Barsauma's blessings and curses now began to be felt in many places: a widespread sickness fatal to cattle was stopped at Harran; the ships by which his party traveled via Cyprus were saved from a storm; a man was exorcised at Jerusalem, where the empress Eudocia showed the saint great respect. The father of a boy with second sight accused Barsauma of envy and was punished by God for his insolence; hail fell at his bidding on the vineyard of another man who opposed him. But as before, his curses were balanced by blessings for his friends, for whom he made a source to well up, saving them a long haul from the river.

The first part of the *Life of Barsauma* culminates in his fourth pilgrimage to Jerusalem, which seems to have been prompted by the report that the empress Eudocia had permitted the Jews to return to that city, a liberty to which the holy man was opposed. On the Feast of the Tabernacles many of the Jews who had assembled at the Western Wall of the Temple died in mysterious circumstances. Barsauma's disciples were accused of murder and imprisoned. But they were vindicated by signs and ultimately by an alarming (though not destructive) seismic event. After the monks' return, a village in Claudias, with whose inhabitants Barsauma had been angry, was swept away by the river Euphrates in flood.

Having told the story of Barsauma's four pilgrimages, the narrator turns to the role he played in the highest politics of the Church. The second part of the *Life* tells how Barsauma was favored by the emperor Theodosius II, who invited him to preside over a synod at Ephesus in 449; and how he was persecuted by Marcian, the next emperor, who called a synod at Chalcedon that reversed the decisions taken at Ephesus. This synod declared that Jesus was one person with two natures, one human and one divine—a doctrine to which Barsauma remained opposed. The rebellious archimandrite was arrested and tried at Constantinople. Barsauma, however, returned, a free man, to the Euphrates, cursing the empress Pulcheria, who died soon afterward.

Even in the remote mountains of Claudias, Barsauma was not safe from the machinations of the Chalcedonian bishops, who suborned members of the local clergy and the military. But many miracles occurred, all of them showing that God was on the side of the holy man. All those who opposed Barsauma or made attempts on his life were punished by God. One day the saint fell ill and lay down—for the first time in fifty-four years. He would never stand up again. Before he died, he cursed the emperor Marcian. After Barsauma's death, which was accompanied by portents, Saint John the Baptist appeared to one of his disciples in Emesa (Homs) and confirmed, before the fact was generally known, that Barsauma's curse had been effective: Marcian was dead.

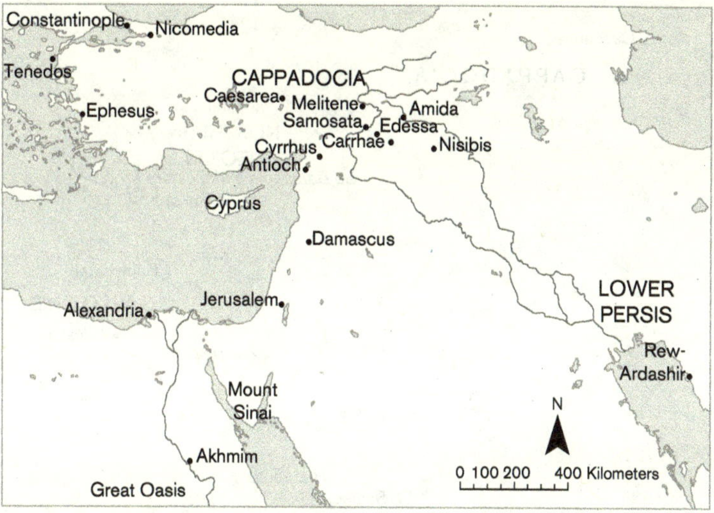

MAP 1. The world reflected in the *Life of Barsauma*. From the Ancient World Mapping Center, adapted by Linda Wheatley-Irving.

MAP 2. Syria and part of Cilicia and Cappadocia in the fifth century. Names in italics occur only in the notes to the *Life of Barsauma*. Eski Kahta is a modern name. From the Ancient World Mapping Center, adapted by Linda Wheatley-Irving.

Overview of the *Life of Barsauma*

This table provides an overview of the *Life of Barsauma*. All numbers, and words not in italics, are based on what is written in the manuscript. Editorial additions are italicized as *Headings*, [*supplements*], and (*comments*). The sections have been numbered consecutively by me, as editor; it is these section numbers that should be used in referring to the text, not the signs, distinctions, and pilgrimages that are separately numbered in the margin of the manuscript. The author seems to have supplied no headings of his own. The lack was felt by users of his book, who numbered the pilgrimages, the distinctions, and the miracles in the margins, adding headings for many of these sections, though not all. Later scribes placed these headings in the body of the text. who divided his book into ten chapters without headings, falling into two parts.

Section	Original structure, as analyzed by editor, and section headings, some added by editor	Signs, distinctions, pilgrimages: numbered separately
	Superscription and Prologue	
Title	The victorious deeds of the holy and chosen Mor Barsauma of the Northern Region	
1	*Prologue*	
	Part I, Chapter 1: Ascetical vocation and first journey to Jerusalem	
2	Revelation to Joseph the Mourner concerning Barṣauma	Sign 1

2.3	*Origins of Barṣauma*	
3	The dogs that bit Barṣauma	Sign 2
	Barṣauma is adopted by a vagrant ascetic called Abraham	
4	*Manner of pilgrimage*	Dist. 1
	First pilgrimage to Jerusalem [*alone as a young man*]	Pilgr. 1
5	The winter ordeal that the young Barṣauma underwent in the open air	Dist. 2
6	The cave that Barṣauma built with the idea that he would die of hardship	Dist. 3
7	Barṣauma's adoption of a standing posture	Dist. 4
8	*Originality of this practice*	Dist. 5
9	The loaf of bread that increased	Sign 3
10	Abstinence practiced by Barṣauma	Dist. 6–13
11	On prayer	Dist. 14
	The tongue of fire that came down upon Barṣauma from heaven	Sign 4
12	Revelation to Bishop Gemellinus about Barṣauma and his fellow disciple Zuṭo	Sign 5
13	How Barṣauma used to go out after the flocks to the Mountain of the Roots	Dist. 15
14	On the bitter roots that became sweet	Sign 6
15	The commemoration that Barṣauma used to make in his monastery	Dist. 16
16	How Barṣauma used to go down to the mulberry-trees in the summer	Dist. 17
17	Hardship endured by Barṣauma from the sun's heat and the burning of iron	Dist. 18
18	The sour wild grapes that became sweet	Sign 7
19	Barṣauma's consumption of food	Dist. 19
20	Barṣauma's custom of prayer	Dist. 20
21	The speech that he would have with his disciples from one evening to another	Dist. 21
22	Nocturnal exertions of Barṣauma	Dist. 22
23	The prayers that Barṣauma used to perform at night	Dist. 23
24	How Barṣauma would conduct the services in the night	Dist. 24
25	Barṣauma's endurance of snow and ice	Dist. 25
26	The demons that came out of a man and his sons	Sign 8
27	The demon that came out of a certain monk	Sign 9
28	The demons that came out of a woman	Sign 10
29	How the sun was held back by the prayers of Barṣauma	Sign 11
30	The pillar of fire and the angel that Barṣauma saw	Sign 12
31	The sign that occurred in the cistern of water (*probably interpolated*)	Sign 13

	Part I, Chapter 2: Second journey to Jerusalem	
32	Second pilgrimage to Jerusalem [*and Mount Sinai with forty disciples*]	Pilgr. 2
33	First revelation to Symeon about Barṣauma	Sign 14
34	Zealous demolition of pagan temples and Jewish and Samaritan synagogues	Dist. 26
35	The rainstorm that occurred in [*Reqem d-Gaya*] the city of the pagans	Sign 15
36	The demons that appeared, attacking the daughters of the priest	Sign 16
37	The pitcher that flowed with wine	Sign 17
38	On the Jewish synagogue [*at Rabbat Moab*]	
39	How he alone routed fifteen thousand Jews who came out to do battle with him	Sign 18
40	The stone that the Jews threw from the wall	Sign 19
41	*How the gates of the precinct of the synagogue opened of their own accord*	Sign 20
42	Barṣauma would not allow anything to be taken from the burning synagogue	Dist. 27
43	How the gold that the thief took was lost	Sign 21
44	The fire that consumed a house of idols [*in the Arnon Valley*]	Sign 22
45	The demolition of Jewish synagogues and pagan temples	Dist. 28
46	Second revelation to Symeon about Barṣauma	Sign 23
47	Third revelation to Symeon about Barṣauma	Sign 24
48	The larder that overflowed in the monastery of Barṣauma	Sign 25
49	The source of water that was rendered healthy	Sign 26
50	The vineyard that yielded no fruit	Sign 27
51	Many [*similar*] signs	
52	The vineyard that yielded no fruit after Barṣauma had cursed it	Sign 28
53	How [*another*] newly planted vineyard withered after Barṣauma had cursed it	Sign 29
54	How an infertile field yielded a crop after a boy forged a message from Barṣauma	Sign 30
	Many similar signs. Barṣauma shielded men from the wrath of God	
55	The snake that dwelt in a monastery	Sign 31
56	The viper that dried up when Barṣauma puffed at it	Sign 32
57	Many [*similar*] signs	
58	How demons took possession of some women who were having fun	Sign 33
59	The demon that left a man by means of a crust of bread	Sign 34
60	The man who was exorcized in the city of Melitene	Sign 35

Part I, Chapter 3: Third journey to Jerusalem

	Part I, Chapter 4: Fourth journey to Jerusalem	
89	Pilgrimage to Jerusalem [*when the empress Eudocia permitted the Jews to return*]	Pilgr. 4
90	Revelation to Jacob about Barṣauma	Sign 60
91	How the Jews assembled [*at Jerusalem for the Feast of the Tabernacles*] and died	Sign 61
92	Revelation to the Jewish people	Sign 62
93	The brother who did not feel the stones that the Jews threw at him	Sign 63
94	The Jewish woman who was shriveled up	Sign 64
95	The five Jewish men who were shriveled up	Sign 65
96	The tremor that occurred in Jerusalem	Sign 66
97	Many [*other*] signs that are not written in this book	
98	The village that was swept away by the river Euphrates when he cursed it	Sign 67
99	The phenomenon of the two rainbows	Sign 68
100	*The water that became milk* (*probably interpolated*)	Sign 69

	Part II, Chapter 5: End of the reign of Theodosius, beginning of that of Marcian	
101	The sweet smell that filled the air, and the angel who appeared	Sign 70
102	Many signs that have not been written down	
103	The death of Zachariah, alias Zuṭo, who became bishop in Samosata	
104	Barṣauma's audience with the emperor Theodosius	
105	How the emperor Theodosius urged Barṣauma to be a father to all the bishops	
106	The letter that the emperor Theodosius wrote to the synod of bishops	
107	On the synod that was assembled in the city of Ephesus	
108	The epistle that the emperor Theodosius wrote concerning Barṣauma	
109	How a certain general, cursed by Barṣauma, broke his bones in a fall and died	Sign 71
110	The sign that was seen concerning the stoning of Barṣauma	Sign 72
111	The false report that certain unprincipled men wrote concerning Barṣauma	
112	How Barṣauma went up to the Imperial City for the second time	
113	How the emperor Theodosius wrote Barṣauma a second epistle before he died	
114	The reign of the emperor Marcian	

115	The bishops' false accusation	
116	The synod that took place in Chalcedon	
117	Dioscorus, the bishop of Alexandria	
118	Mari, the bishop of Qāra(?) in Arabia	
119	How the emperor Marcian sent out a great army because of the schism	
	Part II, Chapter 6: Barsauma's arrest and trial in Constantinople and his release	
120	How the bishops slandered Barṣauma	
121	How the emperor Marcian ordered the arrest of Barṣauma	
122	The demon that came out of a soldier	Sign 73
123	The magistrate who died after Barṣauma had cursed him	Sign 74
124	The prefect whom the emperor Marcian sent to Barṣauma	
125	On the Patricius whom the emperor Marcian sent to Barṣauma	
126	The fire that broke out in the City	Sign 75
127	Barṣauma's departure from the Imperial City	
128	How the empress Pulcheria died after Barṣauma had cursed her	Sign 76
129	The man who was healed by Barṣauma after being bitten by a mad dog	Sign 77
130	On a large number of [*similar*] signs that occurred (*129 and 130 were probably interpolated*)	
	Part II, Chapter 7: Miracles showing that God was with Barsauma against Chalcedon	
131	The fatal contagion that was halted when Barṣauma sent his disciple	Sign 78
132	The contagion that was halted by Barṣauma's prayers	Sign 79
133	The deceitful letters sent by the bishops	
134	The deacon whose withered fingers were healed	Sign 80
135	The paralyzed woman who regained her health	Sign 81
136	The woman through whom a devil reprimanded those who had denied the truth	Sign 82
137	The woman, a Daughter of the Covenant, who was possessed by an impure devil	Sign 83
138	A man possessed by an evil spirit who was healed	Sign 84
139	A preacher who blasphemed and lost the use of hand and tongue	Sign 85
140	A priest who died because he, too, had blasphemed against Barṣauma	Sign 86
141	Another priest who died because he had maligned Barṣauma	Sign 87
142	Many [*similar*] signs	

	Part II, Chapter 8: Attempts made on Barṣauma's life by the Chalcedonians	
143	On the deceitful letters that the apostates sent to Barṣauma	
144	Revelation to a disciple	
145	How the apostates stoned Barṣauma, but he did not die	
146	*How Barṣauma's disciple did not feel the stones that the heretics threw at him*	Sign 88
147	*How something resembling a gale from the east put Barṣauma's enemies to flight*	Sign 89
148	The woman through whom a devil spoke to the shame of the apostates	Sign 90
149	The chorepiscopus who died because he had threatened Barṣauma	Sign 91
150	The tribune who was willing to kill Barṣauma	Sign 92
151	The bishop who died because he threatened to kill Barṣauma (*probably interpolated*)	Sign 93
	Part II, Chapter 9: Last days and death	
152	The letters that the bishops wrote to the emperor Marcian about Barṣauma	
153	How Barṣauma cursed the emperor Marcian	
154	On the vision that Barṣauma saw concerning his illness	
155	The great earthquake that occurred before Barṣauma's death	Sign 94
156	The angel who spoke with Barṣauma and told him about his coming death	Sign 95
157	Barṣauma's death	
158	The pillar of fire that appeared when Barṣauma yielded up his spirit to Christ	Sign 96
	Epilogue (Chapter 10): Deaths of Marcian and Proterius; posthumous miracles	
159	The death of the emperor Marcian	Sign 97
160.1	How Saint John [*the Baptist*] appeared and spoke of the emperor Marcian's death	
160.2	*An alternative version of the same* (*probably interpolated*)	
161	The vision seen by the disciple who made a written deposition to Saint John	
162	*A plague is stopped by dust from Barṣauma's tomb (probably interpolated)*	Sign 98
163	*An enemy of Barṣauma expresses remorse at his tomb and is helped (probably interpolated)*	Sign 99
	Many similar miracles, numbered in one manuscript as "Sign 100" (probably interpolated)	

	Colophons and Subscription
164	*The first colophon*
165	*The second colophon*
Close	End of the story of the hero Barṣauma, the Head of the Mourners in the Northern Massif in the region of Syria

The *Life of Barsauma*

§ 1 The story of the heroic deeds of the chosen one and head of the mourners,[1] *the holy and God-clothed teacher (Syriac: rabbo), Barsauma the Northerner.*[2] *His prayer be with us, Amen!*[3]

1 In every age and in every generation there have been righteous men (Syriac: *zaddīqē*) in the creation; and one righteous man (*zaddīqo*) outstrips another by his love, just as one star outshines another in magnitude; and one champion (ἀθλητής) is as far superior in performance to another as the sun in brightness to the moon.

2 In Barsauma's time there were many mourners (Syriac: *abīlē*), but the perfection (Syriac: *gmīrūto*) of this one surpassed all others; and in his generation many righteous men were found, but his athleticism was superior to the rest. In fact, one might almost say it is unheard of in the history of the world for beings of flesh and blood to perform athletic feats such as his. That, at least, is my opinion.

1. A "mourner" (cf. Mt 5:4) was a monk, distinguishable by his dress and appearance, who practiced extreme asceticism.

2. A "northerner" was a man from the Taurus Mountains; cf. §§ 33.2, 64.4, 68.1, and 155.4.

3. Italics signify heading written with red ink.

§ 2 *The first sign.*[4]

1 The beginning of this man's recognition as one chosen by God[5] was as follows. There lived in the wilderness a holy man, whose name was Joseph. This righteous man lived long ago, before Barsauma's fame began to be known in the world.

2 From his (isolated) station, this righteous man was the first to make Barsauma's chosen status known. He was speaking to a crowd of people who had come to see him. "Mark my words!" he said. "A certain righteous man will soon be revealed to the world. His name is Barsauma. Now the righteousness of this man surpasses that of all his generation, as John the Baptist surpassed all those born from women."[6]

3 Those who were listening to Joseph asked him: "Where did you get this knowledge from? Are you perhaps a prophet?" He replied: "I am no prophet. I saw this in a divine vision." And that holy man used to tell what he had learned from his vision in the presence of all men.

§ 3A *The second sign. Dogs bite him.*[7]

1 This Barsauma, who would be the most excellent of mourners, was born in a village called Beth Awton in the district (χῶρα) of Samosata.[8] While he was still a little child, his father died. His mother, whose name was Sakhiya, became the wife of a man in another village. Barsauma went there with his mother.

2 About this time the little Barsauma happened to be alone one day in a field when some aggressive dogs came on him on their way back (to the village) from the sheep. When these dogs saw that the child was alone, they growled at him fiercely, ran up and seized him, then trotted off again, carrying him between their teeth.

3 The dogs had been dragging him along for some time between their teeth when some men from that village came across the field.

4. Cf. Jn 2:11.

5. Lit. "The beginning of Barsauma's chosenness."

6. Mt 11:11.

7. This heading is written opposite the second paragraph of the chapter, but it belongs here.

8. The village of Beth 'Awton is otherwise unknown. Samosata: Barrington Atlas 67, H1.

When they saw the dogs pulling at the child Barsauma, the men thought they were fighting over some animal.

4 Coming closer, however, they discovered Barsauma on his back in the middle, with each of the dogs pulling him in a different direction. Picking up sticks and stones, they rescued the child from the dogs. When they were close enough to examine him, they looked for the marks of the dogs' teeth, but they could not see even the slightest scratch on him.

5 All this came to pass because of the trials to which the devil would one day subject him, and because of his future struggles with the pagans and the wars of the heresies; for in due course these, too, would attack Barsauma. By this men already knew, when Barsauma was but a child, that victory was his as a chosen one, destined to win all his contests and be delivered from all harms. For just as he fell into the jaws of savage dogs without any harm to his body, so he was destined to fall into deep contests without any harm to his soul.

6 The men who had rescued Barsauma from the dogs stood there in amazement at what they had seen. One of them, filled with grace, made a kind of prophecy: "If I am alive, brothers, I shall remind you. But if I am dead (by the time it happens), you will have to remember what I now say. This child has been chosen by God to be his instrument.[9] He is destined to attain high rank in God's service. This sign which has been seen in him was not performed for nothing." When the child Barsauma heard the man saying this, it occurred to him that he ought to go out into the wilderness.

§ 3[B][10]

7 When the day came for the great fair of Samosata, Barsauma's relatives went into town, taking the child with them. But he left them there in Samosata and ran away, following the course of the Euphrates which flows past that city. And as he walked along the riverbank, he began to weep.

8 Now by the grace of God he encountered there a certain distinguished mourner called Abraham, dedicated to holy poverty (Syriac: *msarqo*). When this man saw the little child, he said to him: "Why are

9. Cf. Acts 9:15.

10. The copyist who added headings to the text omitted to add one here.

you crying? Where do you come from? And where are you going?" Barsauma answered: "Sir, I am an orphan. My father is dead. I want to become a Slave[11] of Christ."

9 Abraham replied: "Where do you mean to go and labor for Christ?" To this, Barsauma responded: "I want, sir, to go into the wilderness, where no people walk."[12] Abraham answered: "My son, you are a child. The wilderness is a very difficult place. You cannot live there on your own."

10 Barsauma was as innocent as a lamb. He believed every word. When he heard this he panicked. He was overcome by dizziness and did not know what to say in reply. So Abraham spoke again to the little child: "Suppose someone were to do you a kindness for our Lord's sake and take you to a monastery! Would you run away?"

11 Then Barsauma answered: "I promise you before God that I shall never stop following the way I have started on." Then Abraham took charge of him; and he went with him. And when they arrived at the next monastery on their way, he urged the monks to accept the child Barsauma.

12 At this the child Barsauma began to weep out loud and said to Abraham: "Sir, if God wanted me to stay here, he would have led me here directly. As it is, it is clear that He wants me to stay with you, because it is you that I first met with." When Abraham heard this, he felt sorry; so he took charge of Barsauma. From there on the child followed him.

13 Afterward other disciples attached themselves to them. These also attained a high rank in God's service and a name in the world. One of them, who had achieved great heights of asceticism by the time he ended his days, performed many signs during his life and more after his death. Amazing powers and miracles are manifested through his bones.

14 This man rose to be a bishop. I could tell a great deal about him. As it is, God has recorded all his victorious deeds in the Book of Life in the heavenly Jerusalem. Eventually Abraham departed from this world, leaving his disciples while they were still young.

11. Cf. Heb 3:5.

12. Cf. 1 Kgs 17:2–6 (Elijah); Mt 3:1–3 (John the Baptist), 4:1 (Jesus); cf. Mk 1:3–4, 1:12–13 ; Lk 3:2–4, 4:1; Jn 1:23; Heb 11:38 (all the holy men of the time before Christ).

§ 4 *The first distinction. First pilgrimage to Jerusalem.*

1 It occurred to the young Barsauma that he ought to make a pilgrimage to Jerusalem. He wore rags of sackcloth, of double thickness, patched together with thick threads of wool and hair. He resolved to wear no shoes, not even sandals, on his journey; to take neither purse, nor bag, nor stick, nor food from one place to another; neither to enter a village, nor to pass through a city; and to accept neither silver, nor bronze.[13] Thus he went and thus he returned, all the way to the East.

2 Now at that time pagans abounded in Palestine, Phoenicia, and Arabia. Christians were as yet few in number in those countries. The Jews and the Samaritans, on the other hand, were rich. They persecuted the Christians of that region. Seeing that Barsauma was a young lad and that there was no one else with him, they beat and tormented him in every place before they drove him out.

§ 5 *The second distinction. He undergoes a winter ordeal in the open air.*

1 After Barsauma had returned to the region of the East, he set out again to go to a certain desolate mountain on his own. He was there throughout the winter under snow and ice. As for food, he received none there from any man, but he would gather the wild herbs from places that were denuded of snow and get nourishment from these.

2 In April he went to another mountain both high and cold. There he fed on grass-roots, until the fruit of the wild trees ripened. For he found some wild trees and stayed there, eating of their fruit, until winter.

3 In the first month of that winter he entered a certain village. Now this village is situated in the high Northern Massif. In that village there were some people who knew his parents. Those people told Barsauma that he should stay there with them. They would build him a monastery.

§ 6 *The third distinction. He builds a cave, thinking he will die of hardship.*

1 Barsauma decided to stay there and build himself a cave-den in one of the rocky cliffs, intending to stay there on his own that winter

13. Cf. Mt 10:5–15; Mk 6:7–13; Lk 10:2–12.

and die of hunger; for much snow falls in that country and then no one is able to go from place to place. For this reason Barsauma thought that, when snow fell in the winter and no one was able to come to him, he would starve to death.

2 By the providence of God, who takes care of everything, Barsauma went and found, in a certain big cliff, a little den in which a she-bear lived; for there used to be much wildlife in that country. That winter he lived in that den. The grace of God provided for him. He did not die. By the summer he had welcomed one disciple and by the next year, two or three more.

§ 7 *The fourth distinction. He adopts a standing posture.*

1 From then on Barsauma began to practice great hardships. It so happened that when he was lying on the ground under heaven and gazing at the stars, fear and trembling suddenly fell on him. He reasoned as follows: "How do I presume to lie on my side, while God is standing and looking at me? If a slave does not presume to lie down in the presence of his fleshly lord, how can I lie down in the presence of the Lord of heaven and earth?" Because of this thought he leapt to his feet and remained standing in fear, offering worship and prayer assiduously in the presence of God.

2 Then he pursued the same line of reasoning: "If a disciple does not presume to sit down in the presence of his master, how can I, weak as I am, sit down in the presence of the Master of All Creatures?" From that moment onward he crucified himself by night and by day. Indeed, he refused to lie or sit down again until the day of his death, a period of fifty-four years.

§ 8 *The fifth distinction.*

1 Now at the time when Barsauma began to crucify himself in the presence of God, he had not heard of anybody on earth who neither lay nor sat down; but from about that time this practice began among the brethren.

§ 9 *The third sign. A loaf of bread increases.*

1 When Barsauma first bound himself to this hardship, God gave him the following sign. In that den in which they dwelt he and his disciples had just one loaf of barley bread. This they placed on the

table on Sunday. All ate of it, and more than half was left. On Monday they put it on the table again, ate of it, and were satisfied; and it remained the same. On Tuesday they put it on the table again. All of them ate their fill, yet it was none the smaller. For seven days they ate of it in this way; and it stayed as it was.[14]

§ 10 *The sixth distinction. He practices abstinence.*

1 After this, Barsauma decided to deprive himself[15] of bread; and—*the seventh distinction*—of wine; and—*the eighth distinction*—of oil; and—*the ninth distinction*—of water; and—*the tenth distinction*—of everything that is sown with the aid of a plow; and—*the eleventh distinction*—he practiced this extreme hardship for fifty-four years.

2 *The twelfth distinction.* He fasted from one Sunday to the next throughout the winter. On Sundays he would partake of some salad and fruit. *The thirteenth distinction.* In the summer he would eat once every two days.

3 He maintained this invariable custom not only in his monastery, but also on the road. Throughout those fifty-four years he did not break his rule. His way of life was the same from the beginning to the end, from youth to old age.

4 It was with reason that this abstinent man was called *bar-sauma* (*bar-ṣawmo:* "Son of Fasting"). From his early youth master Fasting was his tutor; and mistress Prayer was wet-nurse to the child. The prophet said: "My father and my mother abandoned me and the Lord gathered me up."[16] This prophecy was fulfilled in Barsauma; for, when he was young, his father and mother abandoned him, and the Lord took him under his wing. By nature he was still innocent, in speech simple, unschooled in the secular curriculum,[17] but wise in the Lord; for "the beginning of wisdom is the fear of the Lord."[18]

5 [Now because it was appropriate for the following, also, to be fulfilled in Barsauma's case: "God has chosen the fools of the world

14. Cf. 1 Kgs 17:8–16; Mt 14:15–21, 15:32–38; Mk 6:35–44, 8:1–9; Lk 9:12–17; Jn 6:5–13.

15. The verb *etnzar*, "deprive himself," is cognate with the Hebrew word for a Nazirite (cf. Nm 6; Jgs 13:4–7, 16f.; Am 2:11f.).

16. Ps 27:10.

17. Lit. "a layman (Greek: ἰδιώτης) in the learning of human literature."

18. Prv 9:10.

that He might put the wise to shame through them"[19]—and even if this was originally written about the apostles, but it can also be extended to many; and this same thing also happened in truth about Barsauma.][20]

§ 11 *The fourteenth distinction. On prayer. The fourth sign. A tongue of fire comes down on him from heaven.*

1 One day he went, as was his custom, to a certain place far away from the brethren, in order to pray there passionately on his own. Now a certain monk, who happened to be passing (that way), watched him while he was praying. Unaware that there was someone watching him, Barsauma began to groan out loud, shedding tears of profound emotion while he prayed.

2 One moment he was pleading with God with great passion, the next a great light flashed from heaven and came down to earth in the likeness of fire. What appeared to be a bolt of lightning stopped just above Barsauma and was changed. Like a tongue of fire now, it trickled down over his mouth and was swallowed up inside him.

3 The monk was deserving enough to see this miracle clearly. Afterward he walked back to the great congregation of people who were then in that place and told them everything that he had seen. "This brother Barsauma, who is considered by us to be simple and unschooled, has received from our Lord the gift which was given to the holy apostles. So long as I am left standing, I shall remind you (of this): from now on this man's wisdom will be superior to that of all the scribes and teachers. His teaching will be spoken of in distant countries."

§ 12 *The fifth sign. Bishop Gemellinus has a vision about him and his fellow disciple Zuṭo.*

1 Around the same time a certain Gemellinus became bishop of Perrha.[21] Now many were aware that this man had been chosen by the Holy Spirit. On the day of his episcopal ordination, he had a vision from the Holy Spirit about the champion (ἀθλητής) Barsauma and

19. 1 Cor 1:27.

20. This passage—translated literally—is probably an interpolation.

21. Barrington Atlas 67, G1 (Perre). Gemellinus, a contemporary and correspondent of Rabbula of Edessa (see the latter's *Epistula ad Gemellinum*), was bishop of Perrha from 411 to 435.

about his friend Zachariah, who was known among the brethren as Zuṭo. This was before the bishop came to know where they were, for as yet neither of their names was generally known.

2 When he had found them, after making careful inquiries, he examined them on certain profound passages in the Bible; for he was a righteous man, well versed in the Scriptures. When these monks were questioned by him about these passages, each of them gave him his answer; but Barsauma, untrained in biblical scholarship as he was, elaborated a profound interpretation of the Scriptures.

3 The bishop, amazed at the way Barsauma had answered him, addressed both men as follows: "Truly, my sons, you are God's servants; for our Lord Himself, who knows all men, revealed to me beforehand that both of you are chosen." After this he ordained them as a deacons, saying: "You are the first 'sons' whom the Lord has given me as a bishop.[22] I ordained no one before you." From that day onward the name of Barsauma began to be spoken of in the world.[23]

§ 13 *The fifteenth distinction. He goes out, following the flocks, to the Mountain of the Roots.*

1 It was Barsauma's custom to spend the winter in his cave. When the winter was over, he would emerge from his cave-dwelling and go to another mountain about twenty-five miles[24] away from any (permanent) settlement with cultivated land. That place is extremely cold and inhospitable; moreover, the walking there was difficult.

2 From the Unleavened Bread[25] until Pentecost he and his disciples would stay on that mountain in great hardship, eating grass-roots and wild salad; but they suffered more from the bitter cold and frost than from hunger. Indeed, they suffered such extreme hardship that they would faint from cold and hunger and fall to the ground.

22. Lit. "in the priesthood" (Syriac: *b-kohnutho*).

23. Barsauma is called a priest in the proceedings of Ephesus II (449) and celebrates the Eucharist in §§ 49–51, 68, 69, 73, 88 (?), and 96. Zachariah became bishop of Samosata (§ 103).

24. 37 km.

25. I.e., Easter.

§ 14 *The sixth sign. Bitter roots turn sweet.*

1 By chance, while Barsauma's disciples were toiling around in those difficult mountains, they came across a place where there was a little shelter from an overhanging crag. There were many roots there and, although these were bitter, it made a suitable base.

2 When the disciples found out that the roots were bitter, they began to grumble, but Barsauma said: "My sons, you know what it will take to make these bitter roots turn sweet? Just add Christ's praise! That will sweeten them nicely!" That is exactly what happened: from that time until now those roots, so bitter before, have always been sweet.

3 Some foolish people thought it was because they uprooted them year after year that the roots turned sweet; but those who were filled with the knowledge of God discerned that it was because of what Barsauma said that they were sweetened.

4 Now the miracle of the bitter roots which were made sweet by the prayer of the fasting Barsauma is like that of the brackish waters which were made fresh by the prophet Moses.[26]

§ 15 *The sixteenth distinction. He celebrates a regular commemoration in his monastery.*

1 It was Barsauma's custom to come down from the Mountain of the Roots to his cave-dwelling for Pentecost and invite many people there to celebrate an excellent commemoration. They flocked to him from the cities and the villages, from the monasteries and the caves of the brethren and from distant countries. At such times Barsauma would take all the "grace" (Syriac: *ṭaybutho*) which God sent him and distribute it to the poor and to the brethren, wherever they were.

§ 16 *The seventeenth distinction. He goes down in the summer to the mulberry-trees.*

1 After doing this, Barsauma used to go down to a certain low-lying place in which there was a forest of mulberry-trees and there he would stay until the season of the ripening of the grapes. Now the place where the mulberry-trees were was exceedingly hot and oppressive; nevertheless he used to stand there, unshaded, from morning until evening.

26. Ex 15:23–25.

§ 17 *The eighteenth distinction. He endures the heat of the sun and the burning of iron.*

1 Now Barsauma wore an iron tunic next to his skin.[27] He used to keep his face and his chest turned toward the sun as it traveled across the sky, so that his body became roasted by its rays, resembling a fish that is fried in a pan. It was scorched by the heat of the iron, like the skin of a lamb when it blisters in a fiery oven.[28]

2 O molded clod of friable earth, the nature of which is of dust! How much hardship was he able manfully to bear without drinking water! How long he could hold out under the roasting of the sun and the heat of the iron! How heroically he used to persevere, despite his flaming thirst and the burning of the rays!

3 Earth which is heated by the sun burns the grass; and mud which is exposed to the noon dries up in the heat. The flower which has nothing to drink withers from the lack of water; and the seed which has no moisture shrivels in the summer. The tree which is never irrigated becomes parched and ugly; but this rod of flesh which was planted in baptism grew greener from day to day and blossomed and flourished in the Holy Spirit.

4 This mystery resembled the rod of the priest Aaron, which grew green without irrigation and put out shoots without water inside the Ark.[29] Perhaps, too, the following blessing of the prophet Jeremiah refers to him: "Blessed is the man who relies on the Lord and puts his reliance in God! He will be like a tree that is planted beside a spring of water: its leaves will flourish and its branches will be shapely. In a year of drought, it shall have no fear; and its yield of fruit will not be diminished."[30]

5 Barsauma, accordingly, had no fear of natural thirst, because his "roots" were planted in baptism, which does not dry up. Though lacking "irrigation," his yield of "fruit" was undiminished, because Christ's innocent blood pulsed joyfully in his limbs.

6 Again, in not dying, although he was parched with thirst and (burned) by the sun, he resembled the three young men of Babylon,

27. Cf. Eph 6:11, where, however, armor is a metaphor.
28. Cf. Jb 30:30 (Pesh.).
29. Nm 17:16–26.
30. Jer 17:7f.

who were not burned up, although they were roasted in a furnace of fire.[31]

§ 18 *The seventh sign. Sour wild grapes turn sweet.*

1 As soon as the grapes began to ripen, Barsauma left those mulberry-trees and went to another forest on the river Euphrates, where there were wild vines, walnuts, and figs. The wild grapes were so acid that their sourness cracked the brethren's lips and tongues.

2 When Barsauma saw the suffering of the brethren, he said to them: "Let me show you what it will take to make these grapes delicious!" All of them answered: "There is no way these grapes are going to be made delicious!" But Barsauma said: "Let us mix with them the sound of alleluias and the taste of prayer! That will make them delicious!" And that is exactly what happened: the sour grapes became good to eat, sweeter even than those from cultivated vines.[32]

3 Now some of those who were with him, men who were full of discernment, observed with faith what occurred, knowing that it was of God's doing. But others foolishly said: "Perhaps these grapes have just ripened a little more and that is why they are now good to eat." It is a fact that the mystery of these sour grapes which were made sweet by the prayers of Barsauma is like that of the inedible mallows in the wilderness, which were made sweet through the prayer of the prophet Elisha.[33]

§ 19 *The nineteenth distinction. His consumption of food.*

1 This was Barsauma's diet. So long as he dwelt in his monastery, he ate only salad and winter fruit; so long as he stayed among those mulberry-trees, he ate only mulberries; so long as he stayed in that forest of grapes, he ate only of its fruit; and so long as he was on the Mountain of the Wild Roots, he ate only these. If any "blessing" (Syriac: *burktho*) was sent to him, only his disciples ate of it; he did not.

31. Dn 3:19–30.
32. Cf. Rom 11:16–24.
33. 2 Kgs 4:38–41.

§ 20 *The twentieth distinction. His rule of prayer.*

1 This was Barsauma's rule of prayer in the winter. In the morning he would leave his dwelling and go to a place at no small distance from the brethren. No one presumed to go anywhere near that place. There Barsauma would stand with the soles of both feet planted squarely on the ground, then bow down in prayer with his two hands clasped together behind his back from morning until evening. All day long his body was bent double, his head right down beside the soles of his feet.

2 Every day from morning until evening he would subject himself to this hardship. He would begin the morning in prayer, groaning deeply and weeping astonishing tears. The tears streamed from his eyes until the soil in front of him became like malleable clay. So long as the day lasted the sound of his groaning never ceased. At sunset he would bring his prayers to an end and set a seal on his petition. At dusk he would come to his disciples.

§ 21 *The twenty-first distinction. He speaks to his disciples every evening.*

1 When his disciples were seated for their evening meal, Barsauma would enter the refectory; take up his stance in front of the brethren; place a book on the lectern; and begin to read and expound the words one by one, while leaning on the lectern. He read and explained the words tearfully throughout the evening meal. This he did throughout the winter, preaching long sermons to the brethren while they were eating their supper.

§ 22 *The twenty-second distinction. His nocturnal exertions.*

1 After supper Barsauma would go out to that place which had been prepared for him in the open air.

§ 23 *The twenty-third distinction. He prays at night.*

1 He would allow his disciples to rest for a short time, giving the impression of one who was himself asleep on his feet. But his disciples, who used to keep an eye on him, could see that he was actually at prayer all the time.

§ 24 *The twenty-fourth distinction. His conduct of the night office.*

1 Once a fraction of the night had passed, Barsauma would resume his office, while standing in his place. With the windows of the house of his disciples open toward him, Barsauma began the service by intoning one half of the psalm-verse alone; and all his disciples would respond to him with the second half of the verse. His own voice was louder than the whole choir of his disciples. He sang the offices with them until just before dawn, when he brought the service to an end for a short time. Then his disciples rested for a full hour, while he continued in prayer until the morning.

§ 25 *The twenty-fifth distinction. He endures snow and ice.*

1 Now there was much snow in that place. On many days the snow would fall on him until it covered him. The snow mounted up above his head, but he persevered, standing on his feet in the frost and the ice.

2 Now the ice in that place was so destructive that it broke up even the stones and turned them to dust. If a vessel of earthenware or glass was left outside in the winter, it would gradually become cracked and shattered, so violent was the ice and so harsh the frost.

3 O "vessel of baked clay"! O miraculous "vessel"! In what "kiln" was it fired, that it did not fall to pieces, turned to dust by all this hardship?[34] Oh what a profound and unintelligible miracle! Vessels of hard stone and earthenware were turned to dust by the violence of the ice, whereas Barsauma's body, "baked" in living fire and in the Holy Spirit, remained firm and endured by God's power.[35] He gives power to the weak[36] and increases the strength of those who are afflicted with disease. To Him praise and thanks are due, forever and ever, Amen!

§ 26 *The eighth sign. Demons are expelled from a man and his sons.*

1 In one of the villages of that country there was a well-known man of high status who had demons. He, his sons, and his sons' wives

34. Cf. Jb 10:8f.; Is 64:8; Jer 18:6; Dn 2:31–35; Rom 9:20f.
35. Cf. Mt 3:11; Lk 3:16.
36. Cf. 2 Cor 12:10.

were all tried by evil spirits. They brought them to Barsauma and they were healed. From that time onward God began to show great signs and astonishing feats of bravery in him.

§ 27 *The ninth sign. A demon is expelled from a monk.*

1 On another occasion they brought him a monk long inhabited by an evil spirit. The devil called out in a loud voice: "Behold, for many years I have tormented this man and no one has forced me to leave him. But now, on God's orders, I have received this rebuke: 'Do not presume to speak in the presence of my slave, Barsauma!'" After making this speech, the devil threw the man (onto the ground) in the middle (of the crowd) and left him alone. That instant the monk was cured.

§ 28 *The tenth sign. Demons are expelled from a woman.*

1 On another occasion they brought him a woman inhabited by many demons, which shouted out from a distance: "There are seven hundred chariot-loads of us in this woman! Do you want to make us leave her alone with a little gesture, Barsauma the Roasted?" Barsauma answered: "Leave God's creature and move on!" At that very moment they left her and came out.

2 No one can tell the signs which God performed through Barsauma. They are too many to be counted. But even if I am unable to narrate them all, or even one in twenty, yet I must tell a few of that great number.

§ 29 *The eleventh sign. The sun is held back by his prayer.*

1 One day Barsauma left the road in order to climb to the cave in which he lived. In the place where, narrowing his gaze from a great distance, he could make out his dwelling-place he stopped and prayed. His disciples protested: "Master, it is nearly sunset: the Mountain of the Cave is too far for us to go. The walking is hard, the ascent steep and long; and we are tired. Even you cannot do it. Let us rather spend the night here! It is a good place and there is a supply of water."

2 But Barsauma just turned and looked at the sun, saying to his disciples: "Look, our Lord will hold back the sun and tether it to stop

it moving, until we enter our monastery."[37] When Barsauma had said this, he began to walk toward his cave.

3 Now some of the brethren who were with him noted the position of the shadows cast by the sun from the high crags which towered over that place; and the journey of the sun across the sky was delayed. It did not continue in its course, nor did the shadows of the crags move from where they had come to a standstill, until Barsauma had arrived at his cave.

4 When he had climbed that mountain, difficult and long; and had reached his cave and entered it; and had sung a psalm and prayed according to his rule; then his disciples pointed out to each other that the shadows of the crags had remained in their positions. Not one of them had moved. The sun was standing at the same height in the sky and had not progressed in its course, or moved.

5 Then Barsauma turned round and spoke to the sun: "In the name of our Lord, sun, resume your journey!" Like a flash of lightning the sun shot down. Then Barsauma praised God and his disciples followed suit.

6 Barsauma instructed his disciples not to tell anyone about this; and they kept it to themselves and were silent.[38]

§ 30 *The twelfth sign. He sees a pillar of fire and an angel.*

1 Shortly afterward Barsauma's disciples began to carve out some large winter-chambers inside the cave where they lived. Because the foundations of the crag which overhung and overshadowed them were weakened, the whole crag split from the high mountain and was on the point of falling on top of the brethren where they stood beneath it, so that they ran away, yelling. The crag was subsiding by the minute and was on the point of collapse. All the brethren and even Barsauma were deeply distressed.

2 It was night and Barsauma was standing in prayer. From a distance he lifted up his eyes and saw, beneath that rocky crag, a pillar of fire which was supporting that crag and preventing it from falling. The angel of the Lord was standing underneath the lower brow of the crag.

37. Cf. Jo 10:13.
38. Cf. Mk 1:44; 3:12; 5:43; 7:36.

His right hand was stretched out to support the crag, so that it remained standing. Then the angel spoke to Barsauma: "Come back, go in and finish your work! Do not be afraid! I have been instructed by the Lord of All to support this crag and prevent it from collapsing on top of you."

3 Barsauma kept this to himself. Only when he went on a journey and fell ill did he tell his disciples what he had been told. They thought the vision was a symptom of his illness. Yet his explanation was lucid enough. After some days he came back to his cave and found the crag standing as he had left it. Then he finished hollowing out that space beneath it and made there an excellent monastery.

§ 31 *The thirteenth sign. The water-cistern.*

1 The works in Barsauma's monastery continued. Next they began to dig a great pit for a water-cistern. They dug ever deeper into the bedrock. After many days of labor, they reached a depth of thirty spans.[39] It was time for the prayer of the sixth hour.[40] All the brethren came up out of the hole to pray, leaving their rock-cutting and excavating tools in the pit. A small boy stayed behind to examine these instruments made of iron.

2 Now there was a great boulder balanced above the brink of the hole. It had a diameter of about seventeen spans.[41] That boulder suddenly teetered over and fell into the hole. It landed right on top of the boy who had been standing there. The boy was crushed between the iron tools and the boulder. His father saw it happen. He gave out a great wail, then wept, tearing out his hair and flinging it away from him.

3 Everyone present felt a deep sorrow. This was not only because of the boy's death. They were also thinking of all the effort which the brethren had put into digging the pit. "Now that someone has met his death in this place," they muttered, "we will never be able to collect water in it." The brethren went to have their midday rest. After their siesta, they came back to the hole. That afternoon they considered the problem. "If only we could find a way," they exclaimed, "to get the boy's bones out from beneath this boulder!" The rock was too big for them to roll away, so they began to tunnel under it.

39. 6 m.

40. Noon.

41. 340 cm.

4 When they got to the middle, the tip of the boy's foot came to light. Those who saw it wept out loud. At first they thought that the boy's foot had been severed from his body; but when they pulled at it, it did not come out. So they went on digging around it and found the other foot. When they pulled on both feet, the boy came out, firm and alive. Not a bone of his body was broken. He was not even bruised.

5 After this they continued to dig for the tools, weeping and praising God in their amazement as they did so. They found them underneath where the boy's belly had been. Though made of iron, the tools were not just broken, they had been shattered into small fragments. Everyone was astonished and wondered how it could be that hammers, mallets, crow-bars and pick-axes were shattered into small pieces by the impact of that boulder right under the boy's belly, without hurting the boy. The general response was to praise God with loud voices.

6 So they made that pit into a water-cistern after all. But when they tried to fill it, they discovered there was a leak, (no doubt) because it was situated on the top of a mountain. They watched for a long time, but it never filled. Eventually they let Barsauma down into the cistern. He prayed there, then came out again. The same day water fell from heaven and flowed into it, and it was filled—right up to the brink.

§ 32 *Second pilgrimage to Jerusalem.*

1 Barsauma now prepared mentally for a second pilgrimage to Jerusalem. This time he would take forty disciples with him.

2 At that time there was a righteous man called Simeon, who stood on a stone column of six cubits' height in the district of Antioch. Later he would stand on another, of twelve cubits; later still, on one of twenty-four; later still, on one of thirty-six; and, last, on one of forty.[42]

3 But at the time when Barsauma left his monastery for his second Jerusalem pilgrimage, Simeon still stood on the column of six cubits.

§ 33 *The fourteenth sign. Simeon's first vision about him.*

1 Now on the day Barsauma left his monastery for Jerusalem, Simeon had a revelation concerning Barsauma's ascetical prowess. The angel of the Lord appeared to him in the night, saying: "Why do you

42. The first column was 2.4 m high; the second 4.8; the third 9.6; the fourth 14.4; the fifth and last 16.

think that you are the most excellent of the righteous? No one on earth in this generation can compete for righteousness with Barsauma, who lives on a high mountain on the frontier with Armenia. This very day, as it happens, he left his monastery on pilgrimage to Jerusalem." Now Simeon had never heard of Barsauma.

2 When morning came and a large number of people were standing near him, Simeon cried out with a loud voice and spoke to the multitude: "There is a righteous man, who has no equal among his contemporaries on earth. Today he left his monastery in the Northern Region (Syriac: *ar'o d-garbyo*) on a pilgrimage to Jerusalem. I am unworthy of seeing him, because I am a sinner. Otherwise I should have asked our Lord for that privilege."

§ 34 *The twenty-sixth distinction. He destroys pagan temples, Jewish Sabbath-houses, and Samaritan synagogues in his zeal.*

1 So Barsauma set off for Jerusalem. When he reached Phoenicia, Arabia, and Palestine, he began to demolish the Jewish Sabbath-houses, destroy the Samaritan synagogues, and burn down the pagan temples. When he had prayed in Jerusalem, he traveled on to Mount Sinai by the road of the wilderness.[43]

2 Now the pagan population of that region was at that time still dominant. It was they who held the cities. They were afraid of Barsauma; each city shut her gates at his approach. The pagans armed themselves and took up their positions on the wall for battle. Barsauma turned aside and passed by some of these cities; others he overpowered and entered.

3 So when Barsauma reached Reqem d-Gaya,[44] a great city in that country, he found its gates closed and its inhabitants standing armed on the wall. Leaving his disciples standing a long way off, he approached the city alone and cried out to the men on the wall: "Let me come near! Let no one do me any harm! I am the least of all Christians. The others have sent me to you as a messenger to parley for peace." The pagans answered: "If you come in peace, come near and speak!"

43. Cf. § 36.6, where "the way of the wilderness" means the Via Nova Trajana.

44. Josephus, *Ant.* 4.7 (§ 161) and Eusebius, *Onom.* 1447 (s.v. Ῥεκεμ) say Rekem (Jo 18:27) is Petra.

4 So Barsauma came up to the wall and spoke to them in a gentle voice: "You are many in number and have swords, bows, and arrows, whereas we are a mere forty souls with neither swords, nor bows, nor arrows. We have not even sticks, or slings, nor are we mounted. How can we fight with you? There are thousands and tens of thousands of you, all heavily armed."

5 The chief priest of the idols answered: "By the life of the gods whom I serve, one of you will surely put to flight a thousand."[45] When Barsauma heard this, he was amazed and said to that priest: "Do you really know that one of us will put to flight a thousand?" The chief priest replied: "This also I know. Two of you will put to flight ten thousand."[46] Barsauma asked: "Will this come about by the power of God, or by human agency?" The chief priest answered: "By whatever means it comes about, it will be so. That I know."

6 Then Barsauma said to the people: "Your city is built on a mountain with cliffs on every side. We merely request passage through it, because there is no way we can go round on the outside. By all means line the street with armed men to left and right, while we pass between you and go on our way in peace. We shall not even say a single word to any of you, unless you want us to do so. But if you do not let us pass through in peace, we shall make war on you and burn your city down." When the pagans heard this, they were mightily troubled and trembled with fear in his presence.

7 This was what they said: "If you swear by your god that you will neither harm our city, nor burn our gods, we are willing to grant you passage." Then Barsauma said: "If you want, we can speak to you briefly in peace; but if not, we waive even this request." To which they replied: "You may speak for as long as you like, provided your speech is peaceful!"

8 Then the pagans opened the city gates for Barsauma and his disciples to enter. They walked in silence down the middle of the street, and the whole population of the city walked with them to right and left. When they reached the city center, Barsauma took up his stance in the middle and gestured with his hand toward the people, saying: "If you want us to address you in peace, confirm it now and we

45. Dt 32:30a.
46. Dt 32:30b.

shall speak to you!" The whole population cried out: "You have permission to make a peaceful speech; only do not bring evil on our city!"

9 Now the time was about the fourth hour of the day.[47] Barsauma began to address them with terrible words by the wisdom of God and in the true Faith. He continued teaching and demonstrating with eloquent persuasiveness from the fourth hour until the ninth.[48] So powerful and terrible were the words which came out of his mouth that all the pagans were afraid.

10 They cried out: "Sir, we believe that our gods made heaven and earth; but you say that the Christian god made heaven and earth and that it is he that makes it rain and feeds the world. As it happens, it is four years to the day since a drop of rain fell on our city. This city used to drink rainwater from cisterns, because it is built at such a height that no aqueduct can bring water to it. But now the cisterns and the reservoirs are empty. We have to fetch our water from a distant river, which is back-breaking toil. If your god made heaven and earth and it is he who causes the rain and the dew to fall from heaven, ask him to make it rain! If he does, we shall all become Christians!"

11 When Barsauma heard this, his face lit up. He was glad, delighted, exultant. He even laughed out loud. The reason for his confidence was that he had privileged access to his Lord at all times. He said to the people of that city: "Let it be as you say! Just name the hour at which you want it to rain, so that you cannot say later, 'It was our own gods that made the rain.'" They answered: "Make it rain tomorrow at the second hour."[49]

12 To this, Barsauma said: "At the time you have named a great quantity of rain is going to fall on the city, filling the cisterns and the streets with water. If it does not, you have my permission to stone us to death."

13 Then he and his disciples went into a wide courtyard surrounded by high, fortified buildings. All night long armed warriors kept watch around that courtyard, the gates of which were bolted shut. The blessed men sang psalms and were protected from the power of the pagans until the morning.

47. 10 a.m.

48. 3 p.m.

49. 8 a.m.

14 When day dawned, all the pagans assembled near them, from the greatest to the least, in a great crowd. The first hour was soon over.[50] As yet no cloud was to be seen. The pagans began to doubt Barsauma's promise: "Look up there, Christian!" they laughed. "Perhaps your god is a liar!"

15 They were still jeering in this way when the second hour of the day came to an end. There happened to be a clock there. At this the pagans loudly vented their blasphemous contempt. There was laughter on all sides, when someone mocked: "Christians, your god is a liar, it would seem. He has no power to make it rain for us."

§ 35 *The fifteenth sign. Rain falls on the pagan city.*

1 Suddenly, just after this shouting and commotion started, the sound of violent thunder was heard above that city. Terrible bolts of lightning flashed through the air. One celestial salvo followed another in quick succession, an awe-inspiring sound. At this, Barsauma cried out to the living God with the voice of prayer, as the prophet Samuel had cried out with the voice of prayer to God in a rainstorm; and from heaven the Lord, who, with the voice of thunder, had given Samuel his answer, answered Barsauma now with the voice of thunder.[51]

2 All of a sudden clouds came up above the city, and it began to pour with rain. The courtyards, the houses, the cisterns—all were filled with water. In the streets pedestrian traffic was made impossible by the floods. From the pressure of the water mounting up inside the city the very walls were breached and collapsed. Meanwhile, at any distance from the city, not a drop of rain had fallen. Four days and four nights long the violent rainstorm continued.

3 Then the pagans cried out with a loud voice: "Servant of the living God, hold back your rain! Do not ruin our city!" At which God's servant said: "If you want the rain to stop before your city is ruined, deny your false guides, the idols, and confess the God of the Christians!" The pagans cried out with one voice: "We deny them! They are dead! We confess the living God."[52]

50. From 6 to 7 a.m.
51. 1 Sm 12:17.
52. Cf. Mt 26:26–29; Mk 14:22–25; Lk 22:17–19; 1 Cor 11:23–26.

4 Then Barsauma commanded: "In that case, let your priests come out into the open!" At that, the priests of the idols came and stood in the open, confessing the living God and denying the manufactured idols. Only the chief priest still resisted, unwilling to deny the idols and confess God. At this the whole people cried out to Barsauma: "We all confess your God, except for this one man, who is wilfully blind to the fact that his life depends on the true God."

5 Barsauma answered, "As the Lord lives, and as his living Word is true, the rain sent by heaven will not stop until this rebel confesses the God of the Christians." Then the whole people rioted and cried out against that priest: "If you do not deny the dead idols and confess the living God, we are going to kill you and burn your house down." Even this did not make him change his mind.

§ 36 *The sixteenth sign. The priest's daughters appear, pursued by demons.*

1 Now this priest had two virgin daughters, who were being brought up in seclusion. All of a sudden, these girls appeared, screaming while they ran through the streets of the city with demons at their heels. When they got to Barsauma, they were caught up between heaven and earth by their hands and feet, as if with ropes.

2 The demons now railed at Barsauma: "What business have you with us, Barsauma, servant of the Most High God?[53] Have you come here to demolish our temples and to abolish our religion? Ever since this city was built, it has belonged to us. Until now, we received the sacrifices and libations of its inhabitants."

3 When the chief priest heard this, he fell on his face at Barsauma's feet, shaken to the core. Taking handfuls of dust, he scattered it on his own head, then beat his face against the earth, crying out in a loud voice: "Have mercy on me, servant of the Living God!" And the whole people, from the greatest down to the least, cried: "Mercy, angel of light and messenger of peace!" They were trembling with fear.

4 Then Barsauma answered the chief priest and his colleagues: "You must take up hammers and mallets to overthrow and demolish your own false guides, the idols. Otherwise you might say in a few days' time: 'It was not we that overthrew our gods.'" At his word, the

53. Cf. Heb 3:5.

priests all took up hammers and mallets of iron to overthrow the idols and shattered them with their own hands.

5 Next, Barsauma gave the devils their marching orders: "In the name of our Lord Jesus Christ I command you to let these girls be and never to enter this city again." At this the devils let go of the virgins and left the city for good; heaven withheld its rain and the clouds dispersed; and all the inhabitants of that city became Christians.

6 Then Barsauma left that city in peace. In every place he came to he worked wonders; and at his coming every country trembled with fear.

7 So he went to Sinai, climbed the mountain, prayed there, came down again, and returned on foot by the road of the wilderness.[54]

§ 37 *The seventeenth sign. A jar which fills up with wine.*

1 The Christian administrator (ἐπίτροπος) of a town which he was passing came out in great fear to meet Barsauma and his forty disciples and covered their feet with kisses, from the greatest down to the least. It was midday, so the administrator led them to a shady place, then hurried off to his house to bring them a loaf of bread and a jar of wine.

2 Barsauma took the bread and blessed it, then broke it and gave it to his disciples. When he had blessed the jar, which contained eleven pints of wine, he picked it up and put it to the lips of his disciples, urging each to drink his fill.

3 "You are all worn out," he said to the brethren. "You are shattered—exhausted by your journey through the wilderness. Now, therefore, drink of this blessing as if your lives depended on it! Drink as much as you can, then drink some more!" With his own hands he mixed it with water and poured it into their mouths; and they all drank as much as they could, leaving only the dregs. Then everyone took a siesta.

4 While they slept, Barsauma prayed. After praying, he found the jar filled to the brim with wine, so he roused his disciples. They were delighted and praised God for the miracle they had seen. From then until the evening Barsauma was mixing and pouring from that jar. Everyone who happened to pass by drank with them; and, for the blessing's sake, each drank more than he wanted.

54. The Via Nova Trajana.

5 When it was time for evening prayers, the blessed men performed the office there. By the end of the office, new wine had filled the jar. All that evening they continued to drink their fill; and the next morning, when they set out on the road, they left it full of wine.[55]

§ 38 The Jewish synagogue.

1 Barsauma journeyed on through those southern regions, working wonder after wonder, until he reached Rabbat Moab.[56] Now there was in that city a Jewish synagogue unequaled by any ever built, with the sole exception of the temple which King Solomon built in Jerusalem.[57]

2 This synagogue was built of great hewn stones, and its walls and floor were clad in bronze; it was richly decorated with gold and silver, and in all its doorways hung little golden bells; an outer wall of siege-proof stone with great gates of iron surrounded it, and strong doors of bronze closed the house of prayer (Syriac: *hayklo*) within.

3 When Barsauma approached that city, a host of armed Jews, fifteen thousand strong, came out to meet him in battle.

§ 39 The eighteenth sign. Barsauma alone routs fifteen thousand Jews who offer him battle.

1 Barsauma armed his mind against this host and by the Spirit of God he routed them and they fled before him. When he made as if to invade the siege-proof wall which surrounded their synagogue, they bolted the iron gates and took up their positions, armed for battle, on the wall above. Barsauma went straight for the iron gate. The Jews rained arrows and stones on them, but none struck even the cloaks of his disciples.

§ 40 The nineteenth sign. The stone which the Jews threw from the wall.

1 Barsauma and his disciples stopped in front of the gate in the outer wall. While they were standing still, the Jews brought up a great hewn stone and hurled it down on top of them. With a loud crack the

55. Cf. Ex 16:12; 2 Kgs 4:1–7; Jer 13:12.

56. Rabbat Moab is Areopolis, ca. 110 km north of Petra on the Via Nova Trajana: Barrington Atlas 71, B3.

57. 1 Kgs 6.

stone fell on one of the brethren's head; but it was the stone which was broken, not that brother's head. It cracked into four pieces, which fell harmlessly to the ground. The brother did not even feel the blow. When the Jews saw this, they wailed and fled in all directions.

§ 41 *The twentieth sign.*

1 Then, by the will of God, the iron gates flew open. Lifting up his eyes, Barsauma saw the rich decoration of the temple.

§ 42 *The twenty-seventh distinction. He allows no one to take anything from the burning synagogue.*

1 Barsauma said to his companions: "The curse of the living God on anyone who takes any object, however small, from this synagogue! Let this temple and all that is in it be fed to the fire!" Now there was inside the temple a golden ark, a golden table, a ceremonial candlestick, golden torches,[58] and golden lamps hanging on chains. There was also an abundance of gold cladding on the doors, on the walls, and on the columns, not to mention the precious garments made of fine linen, silk, and embroidered linen, the silver, the bronze, and the precious stones.

2 Barsauma's disciples had brought with them naphtha and sulfur. These they made into a number of balls which they hurled at the walls and at the ceiling of the building. All of a sudden fire took hold of the whole interior of the building. It consumed the wooden beams, the stones, the bronze, the iron, the gold, the silver, the valuable garments, the precious stones, and everything which was to be found there. The fire worked its way down to the foundations and utterly destroyed the naos.

3 Now a stranger had attached himself to the blessed men while they were entering that place, disguised in the dress (σχῆμα) of a Christian. While the blessed men were getting ready to throw fire onto the temple, that man stole away on his own. He drew a sword from his belt and laid it to the lower hems of the great curtains which were hung there, with little golden bells attached to them. He cut off a considerable number of little bells and put them in the haircloth shoulder-bag which he was carrying.

58. Cf. Ex 25:10–16 (ark), 23–28 (table), 31–36 (candlestick), and 37f. (torches).

4 One of Barsauma's disciples saw this thief and said nothing; but when Barsauma came out and walked away from there, that disciple went and told Barsauma what he had seen. Then Barsauma summoned the thief to a place where everyone could see him, saying: "Put your shoulder-bag on the ground and open it!" Trembling and shaking, the thief did as he was told.

5 When he saw the gold in the thief's shoulder-bag Barsauma said to him: "Achor the thief treated the curse with contempt.[59] Your crime is just like his! The walls of Jericho were clad in bronze; and so were the walls of this synagogue. Achor the thief treated the curse with contempt and stole a golden bell;[60] and you, like a member of his gang, stole some little golden bells.

6 "Take this darkness, then, which you have loved more than your life, and go and receive your inheritance along with Achor, your fellow gangster!" With this, Barsauma drove out the thief from his company.

§ 43 *The twenty-first sign. The gold taken by the thief is lost.*

1 Having put a little distance between himself and Barsauma, the thief placed his shoulder-bag on the ground and stood there, remonstrating with his loot: "Gold, you murderer and deceiver!" he cried. "What wrong have I done to you that you have separated me from the monastery of the angels? You have hanged yourself around my neck like the noose around Iscariot's windpipe."[61]

2 While that man was standing and weeping for his soul, the shoulder-bag was swallowed up in front of his very eyes and was nowhere to be found. Then that man turned back and fell at the feet of Barsauma, weeping, and told him what had happened. When Barsauma had satisfied himself that the gold was gone, he released that man from the curse; but still he drove him out from his company.

59. Jo 7.

60. One of the objects stolen by Achan (Syriac: *Okhor*, or Akhor) was a "tongue" (Jo 7:21; Syriac: *lešono*) of gold weighing about seven ounces. This is usually interpreted as a wedge, but an object might be called a "tongue" by virtue of its ability to *speak*, hence "bell."

61. Cf. Mt 27:5.

§ 44 *The twenty-second sign. Fire, produced by a stone, consumes a house of idols.*

1 Now one of the disciples from Barsauma's company went off on his own to the Valley of Arnon,[62] where a large house of idols stood, dating from primordial times. It must have been built by the mighty ones after the Flood,[63] because stones of an amazing size had been incorporated in the building. While that monk was a long way away from the house of idols, he took off the habit (σχῆμα) he wore as a mourner and put on the clothing of a beggar.

2 When he reached the house of idols, a great crowd was assembled there. He went in and looked all around the house of idols. Then he sat down among the beggars who were seated in the western courtyard of the naos of the house of idols. From the second hour until the ninth[64] he was with those beggars with his head between his knees, weeping great tears.

3 At the ninth hour, he got to his feet, prostrated himself on the ground, and wept bitter tears with much emotion. Then he picked up a small stone from the ground and wept over it, until it was moistened with his tears. Then took spittle from his mouth on his finger and made the sign of the cross on that stone.

4 Next, so as not to let the pagans know what he intended, he looked up at some birds that were flying beside the naos of the idols and acted as though he meant to throw the stone at those birds. He threw the stone across the path of the birds' flight; but the stone went past them and struck the wall of the naos of the idols and started a fire there.

5 A flame flared up like a pillar of cloud and covered the house of idols. The roaring blaze devoured the ashlar walls. In the path of that conflagration the hewn stones were like dry stubble at the time of the harvest. With the stones the fire engulfed the wooden beams and the statues of the idols, utterly destroying both the idols and their house, right down to its foundations.

6 Not one stone, however small, escaped that furnace. All were turned into a fine ash; and a great wind began to blow and scatter the

62. Barrington Atlas 71, B3; cf. Nm 21f.; Dt 2–4; Jo 12f.; Jgs 11; Jer 48:20.

63. Cf. Gn 10.

64. From 7 a.m. until 3 p.m.

ashes from the burned naos, as the chaff flies away from grain which is winnowed in a breeze. Just so, the ashes were swept off in the direction of the wilderness.

§ 45 *The twenty-eighth distinction. Destruction of pagan temples and Jewish synagogues.*

1 As for Barsauma, he journeyed on toward the Eastern Region, destroying pagan temples and burning down Jewish synagogues.

§ 46 *The twenty-third sign. Simeon's second vision about him.*

1 At this time Simeon addressed a great crowd as follows: "Some time ago I told you about a righteous man who was about to make a pilgrimage to Jerusalem. Well, he has been there and performed great deeds; and now he is safely back, and God, heeding my sinful voice, has put it into his mind to visit my insignificant person and pray for me."

§ 47 *The twenty-fourth sign. Simeon's third vision about him.*

1 Soon afterward Barsauma arrived in the district of Apamea. Then Simeon addressed the crowds who were standing around him as follows: "Anyone who wants to receive a blessing from that righteous man whom I am expecting should stay for three days. In three days' time God's servant will be here."

2 On the morning of the third day Simeon cried out in a loud voice: "Anyone who wishes to obtain a blessing from God's chosen one should stay here until the third hour, because at that hour the one chosen by God will enter this place."

3 Sure enough, during the third hour,[65] Barsauma came, making straight for Simeon's enclosure. When Barsauma was about to enter the enclosure through the gate, the righteous Simeon stretched out his two arms to welcome him.

4 Then Simeon lifted up his voice and cried out: "Welcome, servant of the living God! Blessed was your departure and blessed is your return! Praise to Christ who heeded my sinful voice and deemed me worthy to see your face!"

65. Between 8 and 9 a.m.

5 Then he embraced Barsauma, kissing him on his head and on his eyes. Simeon was not just glad; he was overjoyed and praised God. He persuaded Barsauma to stay for a few days; then the two men asked each other for a blessing, and Barsauma set off for his monastery.

§ 48 *The twenty-fifth sign. The larder in his monastery overflows.*

1 Barsauma was back in his monastery. It was the winter of the same year. One day his disciples entered the larder which they had made and found a superabundance of all the supplies they had in storage. The wine and the olive oil; the lentils and the chickpeas; everything just welled up and overflowed. For eighteen years some residue of that day's blessing lingered in his monastery; only then was it finally exhausted.

§ 49 *The twenty-sixth sign. A source of water is rendered healthy.*

1 The following summer Barsauma happened to be passing through a village with an abundant source of flowing water, which irrigated not only its vineyards and its gardens, but also its plowed fields.

2 However, the villagers were unhappy. "Yes, my lord," they told him, "we have plenty of water; but it is bad. The produce of our lands is diseased and the people in our village die in agony of illnesses. We beg Your Holiness to come and pray over our source!"

3 Barsauma made a shelter above the source of the water, then burned incense and offered up the Eucharist there. He dipped his fingers into the communion chalice and sprinkled some of its contents in the source. At once the water was churned up, and the source grew troubled. An enormous black snake came swimming up out of it before their eyes. It was the poison given off by this snake while it lived there that made the water of that source unhealthy.

4 At that sight, the others all ran away, wailing, but Barsauma ran after it, took hold of its tail, swung it up far above his own height and brought it crashing down onto the ground. The snake burst apart, from its head right down to its tail, at which everyone praised God. From then until now the water has been healthy, like the pestilential water which was made healthy by the prophet Elisha.[66]

66. 2 Kgs 2:19–22.

§ 50 *The twenty-seventh sign. The infertile vineyard.*

1 Barsauma went on his way and entered another village, where the villagers approached him with the following complaint: "My lord, we have an extensive vineyard which we take a great deal of trouble to cultivate—year in, year out. Yet it never produces anything for us to eat. The little fruit that it produces is rotten and crawling with worms."

2 Barsauma prayed in the vineyard and offered the Eucharist there, then gave these instructions: "Be sure to give tithes from the produce of this vineyard to the churches and the poor!" To which the villagers readily agreed. That year their vineyard yielded plenty of fruit; indeed, they could not find enough baskets for the harvest.

3 For three years the harvest was good. But then one of the villagers, a shameless man, began to grumble: '"Why do I give all this wine away and make a loss? Let what I have given up to now be sufficient!" Others heard what he said and echoed his words.

4 It was nearly time for the harvest. The vineyard was weighed down with a great abundance of grapes; and the clusters were of a wonderful size. But all at once, when the day dawned for picking them, the grapes turned rotten; they began to crawl with worms and dropped to the ground.

5 When the people of that village saw what had happened, they trembled with fear. They came to visit Barsauma and pleaded with him. After that the vineyard produced fruit again, but it was not the same as at first.

§ 51 *Many signs.*

1 After this the people of other districts began to take Barsauma to their villages. Wherever there was a vineyard which yielded no fruit, he would pray in it and offer up the oblation there; and it would bear fruit in plenty. In many villages he did the same. Many trees, too, which had been barren before, began to yield fine produce.

§ 52 *The twenty-eighth sign. A vineyard, cursed by him, yields no fruit.*

1 One day Barsauma climbed a desolate mountain to visit a certain mourner. Now this mourner had planted a few grapevines on that mountain. He showed Barsauma the place. "Give a blessing, sir," he

requested, "to my 'novice' (Syriac: *sharwoyo*)—the vineyard I have planted here!"

2 Barsauma was displeased because that mourner's mind was preoccupied with plants. "Praise the Lord," he replied, "who is going to see to it that no one ever eats the fruit of this vineyard!" And that is what came to pass. The mourner has tended those grapevines, pruning, tilling, and propping up their branches, year by year, right up to the present day. But they have not produced a single grape.

§ 53 *The twenty-ninth sign. A newly planted vineyard, cursed by him, dries up.*

1 Barsauma was back in his cave now. His disciples had an idea: "Come! Let us make ourselves vegetable plots and plant a few grapevines there! Then we will have places of refreshment, where we can enjoy ourselves!" So they sent brethren to fetch stocks with which to plant a vineyard.

2 When Barsauma came in from saying his private prayers at the time of the evening office, all his disciples came out to meet him, as happened every day. They prostrated themselves at his feet and venerated him, as was their custom. Then, speaking all at once, they said: "Pronounce a blessing, my lord, over the new vineyard we have planted!"

3 "Bless God's Word," said Barsauma, "which is going to see to it that not one of the grapevines you have planted sprouts! Our 'vineyard' is Christ, who said: 'I am the vineyard and you are the branches.'[67] We are the 'plants' and we will bear tasty 'fruit' through the Crucified, as He promised."[68] The moment Barsauma said this, the shoots of those grapevines dried up and not one of them showed above the ground.

§ 54 *The thirtieth sign.*

1 A good many miles away from his monastery there was a village with poor lands, which produced nothing but weeds and thorns and brambles. The little corn that grew there was deprived of moisture by the surrounding brambles and shriveled up.

2 A certain young man from that village went out into the fields on his own. He selected a smooth stone and sat down and wrote on it,

67. Cf. Jn 15:1–6.
68. Cf. Jn 15:16.

"I, Barsauma, Head of the Mourners, have left these written instructions. If the owners of this land wish to eat of its produce, let them perform a rogation here, then fast and pray for seven days and finish by holding a commemoration of the martyrs at which the oblation is offered. Then our Lord will show mercy and the land will produce enough for all to eat and praise God for it."

3 Afterward his fellow villagers found his inscription on the stone. Believing it was Barsauma that had penned it, they obeyed the written instructions. That year the land produced a bumper harvest; and still the blessing rests on it today.

4 Soon villagers from the surrounding countries began to invite Barsauma to bless their infertile lands and render these productive. Many fatal diseases, affecting people and their animals, were brought to an end by his prayers as well. Suffering people were healed by him in great numbers, and all their ordeals and handicaps were brought to an end by the intercession of the champion (ἀθλητής).

5 To all men he brought all kinds of benefit. Those who loved the earthly would be blessed by his prayers; those who sought the heavenly would find it in his true teaching. Whoever was tempted by Satan would receive help in his ordeal; whoever was being punished by God would get relief from his punishment.

6 Like a siege-proof wall Barsauma stood there, defending the people from God's anger. Like a shield which absorbs the shock of arrows, he protected them from harm.

§ 55 *The thirty-first sign. A snake infests a monastery.*

1 There was a fine monastery in a certain district, where an enormous snake had made its abode. The evil, destructive beast had invaded it, screeching and hissing, and driven out all its inmates. For a long time after this the monastery was deserted.

2 When Barsauma was told what had happened by people from that country, he decided to go there. While he was still a good way off, the snake which haunted the monastery sensed his approach. It sallied out in a rearing rage to meet him, screeching as it came.

3 Barsauma confronted it: "Why so arrogant, cursed enemy of Adam?" With that he took hold of the snake by the middle, whipped it in the air, and flung it down on the ground, where it burst apart from head to tail.

§ 56 *The thirty-second sign. He breathes on a viper and leaves it dry.*

1 Another time Barsauma was praying, bent double, in a place where deep crevices gaped between the rocks, when a huge scary viper emerged from a hole and stopped at his heels, raging and blowing. The snake filled its maw with poison and spat on his face.

2 Was Barsauma frightened?[69] Did he stand up straight when he saw it? No, he fixed it with his eye between his ankles and just blew at it. Instantaneously the snake went stiff and dry, like a stick. His disciples went to the place and saw that shriveled viper, cast down on the ground.

§ 57 *Many signs.*

1 After that everyone who was bitten by a snake came to Barsauma for healing and everyone who was bitten by a rabid dog and came to see him got better. He purged human beings of all scourges and freed them from all trials. In every region he exorcized demons; no one knows the number that were driven out.

§ 58 *The thirty-third sign. Demons take control of some women who are fooling around.*

1 There were some women who came out of a certain village into the fields to fool around and have fun. One dressed up as Barsauma and struck a pose, while the others acted the part of she-devils, screaming for fear of "Barsauma," in mockery of the holy man.

2 All at once demons took control of them. They began to wail and go about with their hands locked together, tearing at their bodies with their teeth. They were still being punished in this way when they came and stood in front of the real Barsauma.

3 Through their mouths the demons cried: "We received an order from heaven to torment these women for fooling around and making fun of you." They went on tormenting the women for a long time.

§ 59 *The thirty-fourth sign. A devil is exorcized by a wafer of bread.*

1 Another time Barsauma was crossing a high mountain when a man appeared, running after him. When he caught up with him, he

69. Cf. Acts 28:1–6.

panted: "Sir, have mercy! There is someone in my house who is at Death's door. When I left him to run after you, they had given him up for dead."

2 Barsauma took a wafer (Syriac: *qeluro*) of bread, made the sign of the cross over it and gave it to that man, saying: "Take this 'blessing' (Syriac: *burktho*) and hurry back home! Place it on that man's tongue, whether he is dead or alive!"

3 Running back home, the man found the patient breathing his last. His nurses had already closed his eyes. But when the "blessing" was placed on his tongue, he took two or three deep breaths and opened mouth and eyes. Then he sat up straight, recovered his vitality, and praised God.

4 Driven out, the devil which had suffocated that man overtook Barsauma on the mountain like a flying shadow. Blowing like a gale, it swept the legs out from under him. For a moment it seemed he was going to fall on his face. Then he stretched out his hands to break his fall—and laughed.

5 Standing in front of him, the devil whined: "Do you begrudge me even the paltry success of knocking you down? I am the devil which was strangling a man in that village over there. You sent a wafer of bread to drive me out."

§ 60 *The thirty-fifth sign. A man is exorcized in Melitene.*

1 The bishop of Melitene in Cappadocia was a certain Acacius,[70] a man both famous and wise. About Barsauma, however, he knew only by hearsay. Now he wrote persuasively to Barsauma at his monastery.

2 The gist of his letter was this: "I beg Your Grace to make the effort to come and bless our city. We are longing to see you." This request was the nub of the bishop's letter, though he covered several pages in saying it. It was enough to move Barsauma to leave Syria and go to Cappadocia.

3 Now when Bishop Acacius heard that Barsauma was coming, he made the following suggestion to his clergy (κληρικοί) and his

70. Barrington Atlas 1, K3. Acacius (Akakios, Aqaq) was bishop of Melitene from before the First Council of Ephesus (431), in which he participated, until his death (after 438 and before 449).

close associates: "I think we should test this Syrian mourner and find out whether what we have heard about him is true."

4 Now there was a man there who had been possessed by a mute spirit for a long time. Every day he visited the bones of the martyrs and anointed himself continuously with the oil of prayer. But the devil remained stubbornly mute. He only tormented the man the more for all his efforts, so that they had to put him in chains. But no iron was strong enough to restrain him. He always freed himself.

5 Secretly, as instructed by their bishop, they brought out this man to test Barsauma. The moment they opened the door of the room where he was, the devil in that man caught sight of the ascetic (ἀθλητής) and screamed: "It is you, Barsauma, the warrior! You will not take long to drive me out." Then, locking his hands together, the man threw himself at his feet.

6 "In the name of Christ," said Barsauma, "leave this body, never to return!" Immediately the devil came out of that man, and he was healed. The bishop and his whole city were overjoyed; and God performed further signs there through his agent.

§ 62 *The thirty-sixth sign. A city administrator, cursed by him, promptly dies.*[71]

1 Barsauma was journeying toward a certain city when some people came from another town denouncing a certain rich man who was behaving badly toward them. They had paid him back what they owed, but he had not given them a written cancellation of their debt. Afterward he had demanded repayment of the debt a second and a third time.

2 Barsauma sent a deacon to summon him. When that deacon presented himself at the man's door, his slaves went in and told him. But the man told them to go back and find out the reason for the visit, so they did this.

3 Now the man did not want to do what was right, so he tried to deceive the deacon. He took to his bed, covered with blankets. When the deacon came in, he saw him there, groaning and shivering as

71. This should follow § 61, as in all the other manuscripts. The scribe of the Damascus manuscript accidentally skipped that chapter and copied the next one, then noticed his mistake and copied out what he had omitted.

though with a fever. He told the deacon to go and tell his master to pray for him because he was ill with a fever; and the deacon reported this back to Barsauma.

4 One of his disciples saw through the trick: "Master, you can be sure that this wicked pillager is lying! He is not really ill. He is just using illness as an excuse so as not to have to come and face you here, where you can plead with him on behalf of those poor people whom he is oppressing."

5 To this, Barsauma said: "If he is really ill and not feigning illness, may Christ restore him to good health! But if he has deceived us, may they take him from the bed on which he is lying to the grave!"[72]

6 With this, Barsauma left; but people from that city came after him. "The man who refused to come out when you sent word to his house," they said, "is being borne, as we speak, in solemn procession to the grave."

§ 61 *The thirty-seventh sign. A city administrator, cursed by him, promptly dies.*[73]

1 One day, Barsauma was approaching a certain city when some poor people came and complained to him about their administrator (ἐπίτροπος), who was using force to oppress them for private gain. Barsauma sent two of his disciples to that man's house to summon him to their master, in order that the case of those poor people might be heard, but he refused to come out to him.

2 The disciples reported back to Barsauma, who duly passed sentence on him; "I asked that tyrant to come out here so that I might plead with him for his own good, but he refuses. God will soon take his soul from his body for this. He will not live much longer to oppress the poor." Word reached him on the next stage of his journey that the administrator had died from a sudden fall.

§ 63 *The thirty-eighth sign. A rich man, cursed by him, dies.*

1 Going on again, Barsauma reached another great city. There was a rich man there, who was the mayor of that city (Syriac: *rishoh da-mdhito*).

72. Cf. Acts 5:9.

73. This chapter belongs before § 62.

This man was a friend of the emperor. The bishops and judges were all biased in deference to him, and he used this power to lord it over everyone. Now this man was committing a great crime in that district.

2 Barsauma sent word to him, and this man did come out to meet him. Barsauma used persuasion, pleading with him to restrain his criminal practices, but he declined to do so.

3 Then Barsauma took a different tone: "By the life of the Lord in whose presence I stand, willing or unwilling, you will do as I say!"

4 At this the mayor was extremely angry. He snapped back at Barsauma: "Rest assured that every word which I have heard from your mouth will come to the ears of the general (στρατηλάτης)[74] and the imperial couple (lit. "the emperors")!"

5 "Will you be going in person to slander me," asked Barsauma, "or are you going to send a messenger?" "I shall go in person by swift horses"[75] was the answer.

6 To this, Barsauma replied: "It is my hope in Christ, whom I serve, that you shall not see your patrons' face, because you have cut off your hope from the true God and have hung it on a spider's web."

7 Hurling angry threats, that man left him. Shortly afterward, driving fast along the road in order to accuse Barsauma at the courts of the general and of the imperial couple, he had a fatal accident. This alarmed everybody; but many could be heard praising God for it.

§ 64 The thirty-ninth sign. A barren woman, after he has prayed for her, gives birth.

1 Barsauma now traveled south. As he passed by a certain opulent town, a great crowd came out to greet him. He had dismissed the crowds and was well on his way again when a woman from the town came into sight. She was running after him and weeping as she ran. At last she threw herself on the ground at his feet, groveling abjectly.

2 "What is the matter with you, woman?" Barsauma asked her. "Why are you weeping so?" She answered: "I beg you! May the god

74. The *magister militum per Orientem* (στρατηλάτης τῆς ἕω), whose residence was at Antioch (§ 109.1), the harbor of which city (Seleucia Pieria) was the point of embarkation for the voyage to the court of "the emperors" (Syriac: *malkē;* i.e., the emperor and his wife) in Constantinople (cf. § 63.7).

75. Cf. Hb 1:8.

whom you serve move you to take pity on me! I have a pain in my heart. That is why I have made bold to run after you. I am the wife of a man from this town. I have no son in the world, and my husband and his parents hate me for it. Every day they curse me, hurl insults at me, beat me. I do not know what to do. Your servant's soul is bitter, afflicted by these trials. Where can I find a refuge from my husband and my parents-in-law? I do not know where to go!"

3 Looking up to heaven, Barsauma said: "Do not afflict yourself with worry![76] Do not cry! It is eternal life you should be worried about. Have a care for that! In the meantime, God in his mercy will console you with a child. The hurtful things your husband and his parents say to you now will soon be a thing of the past." Then the woman left and went back to her house in peace.

4 Ten months later she and her husband and his parents wrote to Barsauma in the Northern Region: "Just as you promised, sir, we rejoice, as we write, in a birth. The child that has been born is a girl. We have called her Bathsauma[77] after you; so pray, sir, for Fasting's Daughter and her parents [*sic*]!"

§ 65 *Many signs.*

1 After this many childless couples applied to Barsauma to make them fertile, and God gave them offspring.

§ 66 *The fortieth sign. An Isaurian causes an outbreak of the plague.*

1 About that time a barbarian of the race of the Isaurians, an uncouth man, was passing through a certain village when he saw a consecrated woman (Syriac: *bath qyomo*). He took her home with him to be his wife and made exchange her habit for that of a laywoman.

2 Hearing this scandal, Barsauma sent eight of his disciples to abduct the woman, intending to have her reconsecrated.[78] The brethren had successfully abducted her and were already on their way home when the villagers came out after them with sticks and stones and took the

76. Cf. Mt 6:25–34.

77. Meaning "daughter of fasting," the feminine form of the name Barsauma.

78. Lit. "so that they might lead away that woman and she might return to her covenant (Syriac: *qyomoh*)."

woman back by force. They did this to please the Isaurian, because they were afraid of him. The disciples then reported the failure of their mission to Barsauma, who responded to the news with the following words.

3 "By the Crucified (Syriac: *ṣlivo*), whom I worship, I hope He will send the Grim Reapers[79] to that village very soon."

4 Straight after that a virulent plague fell on the village. The elders came, hanging their heads and weeping, and prostrated themselves at the feet of God's servant,[80] begging him to forgive their crime. Barsauma accepted their apology and went to pray in that village. The plague ceased to spread immediately after he had prayed there, and there were no more fatalities there at that time.

5 When the barbarian saw what had occurred, he was badly shaken. He took the woman whom he had made his wife, prostrated himself at Barsauma's feet, and said: "Have mercy on me, sir! Forgive my crime! Here is the woman! Send her to a convent to serve God as a nun!"

§ 67 *The forty-first sign. A woman dies, teeming with maggots, because of his curse.*

1 Then Barsauma spoke to the woman: "Take my advice! Go to a convent and serve God as a nun! If this man comes to take you out of there, the angel of the Lord will strike him down on the road. His flesh will teem with maggots and he will die. If you leave the convent and try to go back to him, you will receive the same punishment and die."

2 The woman did go to a convent and stayed there a little time. But then Satan entered her heart and made her leave that place. She was on her way back to that man when the angel of the Lord struck her down. Her flesh teemed with maggots, and she died. This event inspired fear and trembling in that whole region.

§ 68 *The forty-second sign. A disease is prevented from spreading by his prayers.*

1 About the same time a contagious disease fell on a defensible town on the bank of a certain river in the Northern Region. The

79. Lit. "the reapers of wrath," i.e., the angels who are the agents of God's just anger; cf. Mt 13:30, 39.

80. Cf. Heb 3:5.

inhabitants came and begged Barsauma to come with them to their town. By praying and offering up the oblation he prevented the disease from spreading further. All those who had contracted the illness survived. Then he received delegations from the whole district (Syriac: *athro*), for all thanked God, who acts at the request of those who fear Him.[81]

§ 69 *The forty-third sign. A pestilence is stopped by his prayers.*

1 Not long afterward a virulent pestilence fell on a certain fortified town[82] situated in the high mountains of the North.[83] In no time at all three hundred and seventy souls were dead. The elders and the priests came and fell down at the feet of Barsauma and presented this petition: 'Have mercy on us, sir! Pity our people! Unless your prayers come quickly to its aid, our town will be totally depopulated and reduced to a ruin by this pestilence."

2 When Barsauma arrived with them at their town, men, women, and children came out to meet him. The women lifted up their voices and lamented. Every mouth emitted a groan, and from every eye fell tears of bitter sadness. Barsauma, too, was deeply grieved and his tears flowed freely. Raising his voice above their lamentations, he said to the women: "May our Lord have mercy on you and on your children!"

3 He entered the martyrium (Syriac: *beth sohde*) and offered up the oblation there with prayers and the burning of incense; immediately the pestilence ceased to spread. All who were then suffering from it were cured and survived. A great number of people recovered who had been at Death's door.

§ 70 *The inhabitants of the district of Claudias petition him about an epidemic which breaks out there.*

1 In the winter of that year there was a spell of bitter cold, with ice and snow. Such a winter had not occurred for many years. That year would be remembered as "the year of the harsh winter." As if the harsh

81. Lit. "who does the will of His fearers."

82. Jer 1:18.

83. This village was in the district of Claudias, and the plague was stopped there in the month of April; cf. § 70.

winter were not a sufficiently violent punishment, a virulent disease fell on all alike in the district of Claudias (Syriac: *athro d-beth qlawdiyoye*),[84] except for that first town, where the pestilence had been halted in the month of April.

2 The priests and the elders of that district all came together to petition him in his monastery. They made the following address to him: "Sir, take pity on our whole district, before it becomes so depopulated that it cannot recover! As you see, the epidemic has struck the whole district with equal force. Pitilessly, it is wiping out the people. In many a house where it begins in the morning, all are dead by the same evening. In others it begins in the evening, and by the morning they are empty."

3 In response Barsauma said this: "This is a harsh winter, as you know. Many have died of the bitter cold, as you have seen. Many others have frostbitten feet from the snow and ice. Now my brethren refuse to wear shoes. If, barefoot in these extreme conditions, they go with me, they will die. I would come with you on my own, but that is not going to happen. So go and hold vigils and offer up the oblations! Perhaps God will hear your voice and put a stop to the pestilence."

4 They went and did as he said, but the pestilence did not come to an end. So they came again. This time the priests and elders brought many little children with them. They stopped a little way from Barsauma's cave and scattered ashes over the children, who made their entrance first, like a flock of innocent lambs, followed by all the priests and elders of Claudias. They did this so that Barsauma might see the children covered with a sprinkling of ashes and feel sorry for them.

5 At that moment, Barsauma was conversing with one of his disciples, who had been bedridden for a long time with an illness. When this disciple, whose opinion counted for much with Barsauma, saw all those children covered with ashes, he was very sorry for them. He wept and the tears streamed down his cheeks.

6 Then that disciple addressed the following speech to Barsauma: "Sir, our Scriptures urge us to 'Rejoice with those who rejoice and

84. The district of Claudias, on the right bank of the Euphrates gorge, south of the diocese of Melitene in Armenia II, belonged to the diocese of Samosata in the province of Augusta Euphratensis.

weep with those who weep!'[85] When these people were rejoicing, we rejoiced with them. Now that the time has come for them to weep instead, we should surely be weeping with them!"

7 Barsauma was deeply distressed. "You have hurried to the door," he answered, "so as to be the first to open it. For that reason you will not lag behind me. Of that you can be sure." His disciple protested: "Sir, you must be able to see that I cannot go with you in these extreme conditions. I am confined to my bed."

8 "Do you really believe," asked Barsauma, "that God will hear me, if I go and pray in His presence in the country where the epidemic has struck? Will he really stop the disease from spreading further?" "Sir," said the disciple, "if I did not know that our Lord does everything that you ask of Him, I would not have urged you to go."

9 Barsauma pursued his line of reasoning: "So you believe that I, in Christ's name, am going to bring back from Death's door a vast number of people, which is a greater thing by far than healing one person who is neither dying, nor even close to it. Are you not certain, then, that you will get well immediately, if I ask it of our Lord?" "Of this, too," admitted his disciple, "I am convinced."

10 Accordingly, Barsauma gave him this command: "Stand up in the name of Christ and be freed of your disease!" Immediately the disciple was healed and stood up, like one who had never been ill, whereupon Barsauma sang out: "By God, in whose presence I stand, it is my hope that you will see His redemption clearly with the outer eyes of your body."

§ 71 The forty-fourth sign. An epidemic is halted throughout the district of Claudias when he goes and prays there.

1 So Barsauma left his monastery to go to that district. The first town he came to was the capital of Claudias. Accompanied by his disciples, he went into the church of that town. Then the townspeople brought in many people suffering from the disease and laid them on the floor in front of him.

2 At that time there were more than three hundred and sixty people in that place, all of them in dire straits and at their last breath. Then

85. Rom 12:15.

Barsauma formed two choirs of his disciples and intoned the first psalm of the evening office.

§ 72 *The forty-fifth sign. Death, who is Satan, appears with his hands locked together behind his back, worshipping Barsauma.*

1 It was night. Barsauma was standing in front of the choirs, while his disciples sang the psalms. "You will see God's redemption distinctly with your eyes," Barsauma had told his disciple, back there in his monastery; and that prediction was about to be fulfilled. All of a sudden, he had an amazing vision. That disciple lifted up his eyes and saw quite distinctly, from where he stood, the one who, as Paul says, "holds the power of death."[86]

2 There was no doubt about it. It was Satan. He had his hands locked together behind his back. Flames of fire issued from his mouth, eyes, and nostrils. His mouth was open, and his tongue was hanging out like a dog's. He looked like an Indian on fire, howling and panting with the agony of being burned alive. While he was still a long way off, he bowed down low and approached Barsauma bent double, like this! All the time, as he came nearer, he hammered his head against the ground.

3 At last, panting, he got to the place where Barsauma was. The flames of fire which flared from Satan were now beating against Barsauma's habit, now ebbing away from it and curling back on themselves. The holy man suffered not the slightest harm. Satan was bent double at Barsauma's feet, hammering his head against the ground.

4 Then Satan was moving away again, walking backward and bowing and scraping to Barsauma all the while. When he was far enough away from him, he lifted his hands—which were still locked together—over his head, gave a great wail, and fled from the scene.

5 All of this the disciple saw distinctly. At first he supposed that everyone else could see it, too. But when he saw that no one else was affected by what was happening, he understood that by no means everyone had seen it. So he asked one of his companions, who was stand-

86. Cf. Heb 2:14.

ing beside him: "Did you not just see something near our master?" "I saw nothing," answered that brother.

6 "Since you saw nothing," said the disciple, "I shall tell you what happened. Death has just been defeated and put to flight.[87] That means peace, quiet, and redemption for the world!" After that he told him exactly what he had seen.

7 His companion could not believe his ears. Then, between one word and another, in the middle of their conversation, he closed his eyes and seemed to fall asleep briefly.

8 He woke with a start and said: "So what you have been telling me is true, after all! Just now I saw something myself, as in a dream. Our master took hold of a monstrous, savage camel, put three iron bits in its mouth, handed it over to you and two of our brethren, giving you green switches.

9 "'Fall on this destructive creature with these switches,' he said, 'and drive it out. It must be expelled from this region altogether. Chase it over the border into Cappadocia and leave it there![88] Do not let it come closer to Claudias than the village of X!'"

10 What they saw came to pass. The epidemic left Claudias altogether. When it next struck, it was in Cappadocia. The first village in that region where the fatal disease broke out was the one to which the camel was sent in that disciple's vision.

11 Then there raged such pestilence in Cappadocia that many settlements were bereft of people, fell to ruins, and remained deserted for lack of settlers.

§ 73 The forty-sixth sign. The fatal disease.

1 As for Claudias, Barsauma went around the entire district, holding vigils with his disciples and offering up the oblations everywhere. The fatal disease stopped spreading, and the whole district through which he walked was spared. Everyone praised God, to whom praise and honor is due forever and ever, Amen!

87. Cf. Is 25:8.

88. This region included Armenia II (see Barrington Atlas 1, J–K3), which shares a border with the district of Claudias (§ 70).

§ 74 *The forty-seventh sign. A disciple sees a wonder beside him in the night.*

1 It was night. Barsauma had returned, to his cave in peace. He was standing outside the oratory of his disciples and singing a psalm with them. He intoned each verse on his own, and they responded with the second half. Thick snow was falling on him. A great storm-wind was roaring.

2 Inside the oratory, performing the night office with his brethren, was the disciple who had had the first vision of death. He was distressed for Barsauma. What a gale he was standing in! What a contest he was engaged in! What extreme conditions he was enduring!

3 The disciple began to pray: "Our Lord Jesus Christ, what sin has he committed against You? This man loves You. He stays on his feet night and day, sustained by the hope which You have given him. Why should he, of all people, get such a beating in Your presence?

4 "Tortured by frost, seared by ice, snow devours, gales gnaw at him. He struggles to stay awake, yet tires himself out with prayer. Broiled by fasting, scorched by thirst, he keeps up the fight, though agony saps his strength. Burned by iron, tormented by sackcloth, all night he groans, all day he moans. Why do You make him go through this? He loves You with all his heart!"

5 In answer to the disciple's prayer, the Lord opened his eyes and ears. All at once he saw a glorious sight and heard the sound of praise from many mouths. Out of the oratory window he saw a bright light around Barsauma and heard a massed choir of angels loudly intoning the psalm with him.

6 At this he shook and shuddered and fell down on his face. He had supposed that all his brethren could see what he saw. When he saw them standing serenely in the order of their ranks, he realized that he was the only one who could see it.

§ 75 *The forty-eighth sign. A seraph is seen collecting his tears while he weeps in prayer.*

1 The next day Barsauma was praying at a distance from the brethren, since it was not yet time for the evening office, when one of his disciples happened to see him at his prayers, bent double with his hands clasped behind him, as was his custom.

2 A seraph from heaven stood facing him with two of its wings extended under his face. With one it collected his tears as they fell from his eyes, with the other it wiped away their traces. For a long time it remained with him like this.

3 At last Barsauma straightened himself and brought his prayers to a close with the sign of the cross, whereupon the seraph put two of its wings around his neck, raised the soles of its two feet from the ground, floated up, and stood on his shoulders.

4 When he began to walk away from that place, the seraph raised the soles of its feet again and stood on his head. Then, suddenly, it changed into a cross of light and flew up off his head into heaven.

§ 76 *The forty-ninth sign. Third pilgrimage to Jerusalem. The cattle-killing disease.*

1 Later, after the necessary mental preparations, Barsauma made his third pilgrimage to Jerusalem. After many days on the road he reached the opulent town of Carrhae.[89] The inhabitants of this town came out to meet him, carrying thuribles with incense and lamps.

2 They made a communal address to him: "Sir, we beg you to help us! A disease fatal to cattle is spreading throughout this region. It fells livestock as a reaper cuts corn. Where it strikes not a single animal survives for miles around."

3 Barsauma gave them this assurance: "I have confidence in Christ, whom I am going to worship in Jerusalem, that not a single head of the cattle belonging to this town will be lost in this epidemic." Then he blessed them and went on his way in peace.

4 The great pestilence swept through that country, and all the cattle died. But in that town not one head was lost, a remarkable fact which was soon generally known.

§ 77 *The fiftieth sign. The cattle-killing disease, again.*

1 At that time the disease which killed cattle had broken out in many countries. This epidemic spread from the capital of Lower

89. According to the *Peutinger Map* "Charra" (Ḥarran: Barrington Atlas 89, B4), south of Edessa, was reached from Samosata via the Euphrates crossing at Zeugma, making it nearly a fortnight's journey by Roman road from Barsauma's monastery. From Carrhae, Barsauma will have traveled via Batnae and Hierapolis to Laodicea, from which port he sailed to Cyprus.

Persis[90] all the way to the islands in the Western Sea, which belongs to the Romans.

2 "There is no one who has the power to check the epidemic," it was revealed to men, "except for Barsauma who dwells in the Northern Massif. God has given authority to him alone to stop the disease which kills animals, domestic and wild, and even people."

3 Because of this revelation, made to many in dreams and visions, people from every country converged on Barsauma as he traveled along the road and requested his help in combatting this disease.

4 He sent them all on their way with the oil of prayer, which kept the epidemic away from them. If someone had a revelation about him and the people of that village went to see him, all their cattle survived. Conversely, where people ignored the revelation, all their cattle were lost.

§ 78 *The fifty-first sign. Signs occur at sea.*

1 Barsauma, accompanied by one hundred brethren, went to Laodicea and took ship for Cyprus. After disembarking on that island[91] the monks were assigned benches on two ships, one group being separated from Barsauma. His rule, incidentally, was the same at sea as on dry land. To the end of his life he never sat or lay down.

2 At sea a great storm broke, and many ships were lost. As for the ship on which Barsauma was standing, the waves passed over her and hid her from view, but no water fell inside the ship.[92] The waves were spread out over that ship like a tent.[93]

3 Flat on their faces at his feet, his disciples wept. Then one of them looked up to heaven and saw a lady wearing purple. She flew down close to the ship. "Give glory to God," she called, "and you will escape, safe and sound, from the sea!"

4 Another disciple looked up to heaven and saw a tent-peg fixed in the sky. Three flaxen ropes, secured to that stake, had been thrown down onto the ship's deck.[94]

90. The capital of Fars was Rew-Ardashir (Arabic: Reishahr), on the northeast coast of the Persian Gulf.

91. Presumably at Salamis: Barrington Atlas 1, J3.

92. Cf. Jon 2:3, 5; Ex 14:22.

93. Cf. Ex 40:34.

94. Cf. Is 33:20.

5 The disciple who had the first vision now looked out to sea. There, large as life, on the surface of the water, were two angels, striding ahead, hauling the ship along with white ropes. Each held a staff of cornelian in his other hand and with these they subdued the waves in the ship's path. From then on no wave arched right over the ship, yet it still blew a raging gale.

6 At dawn, Barsauma said his prayers, then intoned the first of the morning psalms of praise. With the first note that came out of his mouth, the wind dropped and the din of the storm died away.

7 The ship's captains still thought they were doomed. "That is it, then," they said. "We shall never return to civilization (Syriac: *l-athro d-shayno*). We are doomed to fall where the Outer Ocean goes steeply downward."[95]

8 Then Barsauma's disciples looked up and saw a bird flying toward them just above the surface of the sea; and that bird had a crown of cornelian on its head.

9 It circled the ship three times, then turned back in the direction from which it had come. At this the ship changed course and turned to follow the bird. "This is no ordinary bird," said one of the brethren. "It is a sign of peace sent by God. We are going to reach land safe and sound."

§ 79 *The fifty-second sign. A Jew has a vision of him.*

1 Meanwhile, the other ship, in which half of Barsauma's disciples were seated, was on the point of sinking, swamped by wave after towering wave.

2 In spite of the tempest which the ship was riding, one of the ship's captains dozed off briefly. All of a sudden, this man started up and shouted to the brethren: "Which of you has a ruddy complexion and wears an iron tunic under sackcloth?" They answered: "That is our master's description! He is in the other ship with the rest of the monks."

3 Now that man was a Jew from a distant country who had no idea of Barsauma's appearance. He said: "I had a dream just now. A man was running across the sea, intent on sinking our ship, when another with a ruddy complexion, wearing an iron tunic under

95. Lit. "We have fallen within the descent (*maḥḥatto*) of Okeanos." Cf. Mi 1:4; Acts 27:17 (Pesh): "the descent (*maḥḥatteh*) of the sea."

sackcloth, strode out from among us to confront him, saying: 'This ship belongs to me. You have no right to touch it.'

4 "The first man answered him: 'At sea I have great authority and I intend to sink this ship.' 'I, too, have authority,' said the man wearing the iron tunic, 'on land and in heaven and at sea. Everywhere, in fact. And my authority is greater than yours.' At this, the killer took to his heels."

5 So both ships came safe and sound to harbor. As for the Jew, he was converted to Christianity.

§ 80 *The fifty-third sign. A Samaritan woman is healed.*

1 In the region of Palestine there lies a city called Sebastia.[96] It was noon and Barsauma was waiting in the shade of an aqueduct to enter this city, when a teacher of the Law (of Moses), a Samaritan, engaged him in debate.

2 Refuted from the text of the Law, the Samaritan raised the stakes: "My wife is confined to her bed with a fatal illness. She does not have long to live. If you can demonstrate that your doctrine is true by healing my wife with your prayers, then we shall both become Christians and so will my children!"

3 "Give me the palm of your hand," said Barsauma. "Take the oil I am going to give you and anoint your wife! If that does not heal her, what I teach is a falsehood."

4 "How can I accept oil from you?" the Samaritan protested. "It is unlawful for Samaritans to deal with Christians." But Barsauma persuaded him at last, and he went home with the oil of prayer and anointed his wife, who recovered instantaneously and acknowledged the Messiah.

5 The man brought his wife and children to see Barsauma. He threw himself at his feet, sobbing, and the whole family became Christians. Many others also came to see him; he spoke with them about the whole truth and performed many miracles there.

§ 81 *The twenty-ninth distinction. His refusal of gifts and his instructions to the brethren.*

1 In that country they brought him many gifts, but he refused to accept anything but food and drink for the brethren.

96. Samaria-Sebaste: Barrington Atlas 69, B5.

2 In his own monastery and the district where it lay Barsauma's rule was to accept everything that was offered to him. But when he left his monastery and went on a journey, he accepted food and drink, but nothing else, neither gold, nor silver, nor bronze, nor clothes.

3 What is more, he had put all his disciples under a solemn obligation not to accept anything from anyone behind his back.

4 When his disciples were passing between grapevines, or through gardens, he allowed no one to stretch out his hand to pluck of the fruit and eat; and they kept this rule on their journeys as long as he lived.

§ 82 *The fifty-fourth sign. He expels a devil from a man in Jerusalem.*

1 Barsauma traveled on to Jerusalem. As soon as he got there, he went to the great church which was erected over Golgotha and prayed in our Redeemer's tomb.[97]

2 He took up lodgings at a monastery beside the basilica (Syriac: *hayklo*) of Sion[98] and returned secretly after nightfall to pray in the courtyard of the Golgotha church. Now many people were sleeping in that courtyard, in one of whom lurked an unclean spirit.

3 All of a sudden this devil cried out in a loud voice: "I know you are Barsauma, the warrior! Why have you come in like a thief against me? Do you mean to expose me and expel me from this man?"

4 "Shut your mouth," snapped Barsauma, "and be quiet! Do not speak! In Christ's name, leave this man!" The demon left without a word, and the man was healed.

§ 83 *The thirtieth distinction. He refuses the gifts which the empress Eudocia offers him.*

1 Now it so happened that the empress Eudocia was also visiting Jerusalem at that time.[99] She had heard such reports about Barsauma that she sent him a great quantity of gold. He refused the gift.

97. The Church of the Holy Sepulchre (Greek: *Anastasis*). It was built by Constantine, beginning in 326.

98. Cf. §§ 95.4; 96.11.

99. The empress Eudocia, consort of the emperor Theodosius II, first visited Jerusalem in the spring of 438 or shortly afterward in thanksgiving for the marriage of her daughter Eudoxia to the Western emperor Valentinian III on 29 October 437.

2 She then sent him a long letter, requesting an interview; so he came to see her and he spoke with her at length.

3 Afterward she prostrated herself at his feet, saying: "Sir, if you know any way by which your servant may live, do not keep it from me! I implore you, show me the way which leads to salvation!"

4 "I know what I shall say to you," he answered. "I shall say what Daniel said to King Nebuchadnezzar of Babylon: 'Pay for your sins with almsgiving and for your wickedness with mercy for the weak!'"[100]

5 "How can almsgiving redeem me from my sins?" the empress replied. "After all, it is not from the work of my hands that alms will be given.

6 "The martyrs offered their bodies as a sacrifice to God and reconciled him by their physical sufferings. Those who hold vigils and keep fasts give glory to God from the labor of their bodies; indeed, the labor of their bodies is considered equivalent to the agonies of the martyrs.

7 "All the poor, the orphans, and the widows offer the abasement and distress of their bodies to God as a sacrifice; when they give a morsel of bread to others in faith, the sacrifice of their hands is acceptable in heaven, because they give it from the labor of their bodies.

8 "As for me, however much I want to give, my alms will not be given at the cost of my own body's discomfort, but at the cost of the labor and the exhaustion of the poor. My alms will not come out of what I myself need, like those of a pauper, but out of an excess of wealth.

9 "If a poor man gives a little of what he needs, he will go short. But I, even when I have given much, shall lack for nothing. In what way does my almsgiving resemble that of a distressed widow, who has earned a loaf of bread with the labor of her hands and gives half to one poorer than herself?"

10 When Barsauma heard this, he was amazed. "This is the way I see it," he replied. "It is written in the Gospel of Christ that the Son of Man will come in his glory and sit on the throne of his majesty.

11 "Then all the inhabitants of the earth shall assemble in His presence; and He will separate one from another, as a shepherd separates the sheep from the goats. He will make the lambs stand on his right and the goats on his left.

100. Dn 4:27.

12 "The King will open his mouth and say to those righteous ones on his right: 'Come in peace, blessed ones of the Father! Enter and inherit the Kingdom which has been prepared for you from the beginning!

13 "'For I was hungry and you gave me to eat, thirsty and you gave me to drink; I was a foreigner and you welcomed me, naked and you clothed me; I was sick and you nursed me, in prison and you visited me.'[101]

14 "Now none of these promises are for the martyrs, nor for those who fast, nor for those who mourn, nor for the poor; they were all made to those who do good and give alms.

15 "It is well known which promises have been made to the martyrs and to those who fast; and something else again has been promised to the poor. Our Lord did not say to those righteous ones: 'You fasted,' or 'You kept vigil,' or 'You were persecuted,' or 'You were impoverished.'

16 "As for those on the left, on whom He said there was a curse, and whom He sent into the fire which is never extinguished, He did not send them into the fire because of the number of their sins, but because, while possessing all good things themselves, they did not alleviate the lot of the poor.

17 "Perhaps those sinners even had other works which were good. But because they did not nourish the poor, their other works, however good, were not accepted. Their good works were deprived of their just reward because of their lack of mercy.

18 "As for the righteous ones who inherited the Kingdom of Heaven, they may have had shortcomings as well. But those shortcomings were overlooked because of the compassion they showed to unfortunate people.

19 "After all, the Kingdom of Heaven is promised to the poor. Did not our Lord say, 'Blessed are the poor in spirit, for theirs is the Kingdom of Heaven!'[102]

20 "For the rich, on the other hand, there is unhappiness in store. Did not our Redeemer say in his Gospel: 'You rich people have nothing good to look forward to. You have already received your consolation!'[103]

101. Mt 25:33–36; the following passage continues to refer to Mt 25:31–46.

102. Mt 5:3.

103. Lk 6:24.

21 "But then again, our Redeemer added this: 'Blessed are the merciful, for they shall obtain mercy!'[104] So if the rich act mercifully toward the poor, they will be spared the misfortune which had been prepared for them. Together with the poor, they will inherit the Kingdom which is prepared for them. God is not unjust: He will not leave out of account the alms which are given in faith by the wealthy."

22 When the empress Eudocia heard this, she began to grovel at Barsauma's feet, shedding bitter tears. "My lord," she sobbed, "I thought there was no way for me to be saved. I have committed so many sins, I have lost count of them.[105]

23 "Now that I have it on your unerring authority, that there is indeed hope for sinners such as me, I shall practice this virtue with all my strength. I understand that this is the way for me to earn salvation."

24 From that day onward the empress began to give charitable gifts to the poor in plenty. She continued to do so all the days of her life.

25 She urged Barsauma forcefully to accept some gift from her, but he refused.

26 Barsauma was already near the door of her house and about to leave, when she took hold of his cloak. "Since you refuse to accept a gift from me, a sinner, a gift of which you have no need, leave your cloak for me! I want it—I *need* it to obtain salvation!"

27 So she took from him the cloak which had been wrapped around him and draped it beside her as a blessing. Only then did she let him leave her house.

28 As soon as Barsauma had set out on his journey back home, she took her own precious veil and sent it to him with the following message, to which she added great oaths: "Do not reject this small blessing which your servant has offered to the altar of your God. That would break my heart.

29 "I have not sent anything to you personally, because you have shut the door of your will in my face, as we both know. I have only sent a small offering to you as to a priest of God. So please offer it to God, like a true priest, on my behalf. God's door, after all, is open to sinners!"

104. Mt 5:7.

105. Late in 441 or early in 442 the empress Eudocia withdrew from Constantinople to the Holy Land, perhaps because of rumors that she had committed adultery. These rumors date from after her first pilgrimage.

30 Now Barsauma was deeply troubled because she had used the name of God to force his hand; but in consideration of her oaths, he overcame his reluctance and accepted the veil, which he would adapt to the service of God's altar.

§ 84 The fifty-fifth sign. A Samaritan boy is healed.

1 On his way home Barsauma again passed through Samaria. He happened to be in a certain village on the Sabbath Day, and all the inhabitants came to see him. They disputed with him about the resurrection of the dead and the Son of God, both of which they denied, as they denied the existence of the Holy Spirit and the angels.

2 Barsauma disputed with them on the basis of the Law of Moses, because the Samaritans do not accept any other Scripture. He went through the Law word by word, from the beginning to the end, proving his point to them.[106]

3 When the Samaritans found their tenets refuted from the Law of Moses, they resorted, with one accord, to the following proof: "Look, there is a boy here who is on his death-bed. His fate has been sealed. If you can bring this boy back to life, we will believe in your Christ and in the resurrection of the dead."

4 Barsauma gladly accepted this challenge. The boy was fetched, and Barsauma went up to him and took hold of his hand, saying: "In the name of the Christ whom I worship, I command you, child, arise!" Instantly, the boy opened his eyes, revived, and arose, his health restored.

5 That evening his father joined the brethren, standing between their choirs, with that boy holding his right, his brother his left hand and another son on his shoulders.

6 Seeing this, Barsauma remarked: "What this Samaritan has done is like that passage in the Prophets, where it says, 'Behold, I and the sons whom the Lord has given me!'"[107] Many other Samaritans in that place also became Christians because of what had happened there.

106. Cf. Mk 12:18–26.
107. Is 8:18.

§ 85 *The fifty-sixth sign. Crowds come out to meet him, and he stops a cattle epidemic.*

1 Traveling on toward the East, Barsauma was given a festive escort in the cities and villages of every district he passed through. At the boundary of each city's territory, its bishop, its judge, and a vast crowd of people were waiting to make him welcome. He performed many signs which are not written in this book before arriving back, safe and sound, at his monastery.

2 Thus the whole region of Syria was filled with joy at his coming. But many came to him from other regions as well because of the epidemic which was destroying the cattle everywhere; and wherever Barsauma's writ ran, the sickness was arrested.

§ 86 *The fifty-seventh sign. The clairvoyant boy.*

1 There was a certain small boy in a certain village who was possessed by a spirit of clairvoyance. He told people's fortunes; and his predictions were frequently correct. People came to him from far and near and to each he told his future. Even priests and learned men were led astray by him, for they thought that he prophesied by the inspiration of the Holy Spirit. But when Barsauma heard, he said: "This boy does not prophesy by the Holy Spirit, but by the spirit of Satan."

2 Now Barsauma happened to go through the village where that fortune-teller lived; so he summoned the boy's father. "My son," he told him, "do not let Satan trick you into doing his will! As for your wretched son, he is possessed by a fortune-telling demon." At this the man boiled with anger: "Do not be envious of my son," he said, "just because his celebrity is equal to your own! This country is big enough for both of you."

3 Barsauma retorted: "Is that what you think of me, son of perdition? That I am consumed with envy?" "It is plain to see," the man answered back, "that envy has made its home in you." "If I say this to you out of envy," Barsauma snapped, "may the lance of the Lord be directed straight at me! But if I have spoken to you in love, you will soon pay the penalty."

4 The very next day—Barsauma had gone to another village—the man's fellow villagers came to him. "My lord," they said, with tears in their eyes, "that man whom you cursed yesterday evening fell down and burst open in the night. We buried him first, then came to see you.

The boy who used to tell people's fortunes and his brother are coming after us. They, too, are weeping."

5 When those two boys caught sight of Barsauma from a distance, a demon took control of one of them and he began to cry out as he came nearer. When they both caught up with him, the other boy's demon lifted him off the ground and dropped him there in front of Barsauma. Then both of the evil spirits yelled as one: "We are spirits of fraudulence with the outward appearance of truthfulness. But your presence, Barsauma, is like the furnace in which metal is shown to be debased."

6 By way of answer Barsauma barked a command: "Come out of these boys in the name of Christ!" Instantly, the unclean spirits came out of them and they were healed.

§ 87 The fifty-eighth sign. Hail falls from heaven.

1 Now Barsauma lived on the lands of a certain village, where he had friends. He had given these friends some advice which was meant in a good way. But somehow the advice had given them the impression that he wanted to harm them in some way.

2 The next day Barsauma left his monastery and went to the vineyard of those friends. While he was still a long way off, he called the brethren who were with him to witness: "In a moment I am going to ask our Lord to give me a sign of his favor. The moment we enter that vineyard over there, I am going to pray for a sign. I shall pray for much hail to fall, but only in a circle around the vineyard, not further off, while the vineyard itself remains undamaged. Then the owners will know that my intentions toward them are good."

3 Then Barsauma entered the vineyard, and as yet there was no cloud in the sky. But when he bent double in prayer, there was a great clap of thunder directly above it and the vineyard was encircled with cloud, like a sheepfold. Suddenly great stones of hail were pelting down, but only just outside the vineyard fence. Inside nothing bad happened, nor did a single stone fall further off.

4 At this the owners, who had been standing next to him, prostrated themselves at his feet, abjectly weeping. As for Barsauma, he exulted. A quantity of hail had piled up outside the wall. "That should convince you," Barsauma said, "that my intentions toward you are good." From then on those people were like good slaves to him, dedicated, body and soul, to his service.

§ 88 *The fifty-ninth sign. A new source begins to flow.*

1 There was a certain large village where they had great faith in him and held him in high regard. Consequently, Barsauma had a great love for that particular village. One day, when he came to visit them, the villagers, from the greatest to the least, gathered around him in vast numbers, while he preached to them, as was his custom, the word of God.

2 Afterward the people raised the following matter: "Sir, this village is populous and rich in livestock. But there is no water nearby. We draw our water from a deep river-gorge. This is exhausting work, both for the people and for their beasts of burden."

3 "Are you not able," Barsauma inquired, "to dig wells?" "We cannot find any water here," they replied, "because our village is situated on a high mountain." On hearing this, Barsauma asked: "Where would be the most suitable place for a source?" They said that where they happened to be standing would be just the place. Then God's Slave[108] said: "Let everyone leave this place!" So they all moved back.

4 Barsauma then knelt down on the dry earth and prayed. When he had finished his prayers and was preparing to go, all of a sudden a source was opened and began to well up in that place. After blessing the water, which was already gushing out in plenty, Barsauma scooped up a palmful of it—the firstfruits, as it were—and poured it into the chalice of the oblation. Then everyone came and partook of that water. This miracle caused general rejoicing, and everyone praised God.

§ 89 *His fourth pilgrimage to Jerusalem.*

1 Soon after this there was great commotion in the city of Samosata on account of what the empress Eudocia had done, and Barsauma left for Jerusalem in order to be near the empress, who was there. All Syria and Palestine were in commotion, too. Even the emperor Theodosius came to hear of it.

108. Cf. Heb 3:5.

§ 90 *The sixtieth sign. The righteous Jacob has a revelation.*

1 When Barsauma came to Cyrrhestica[109] on his way to Antioch, the righteous man who resided[110] next to the city of Cyrrhus[111] sent his representatives to meet him. So Barsauma visited him and was joyfully received by him. That night Barsauma stayed with him.

2 Barsauma was leaning (on his staff), asleep on his feet, when Jacob suddenly looked up and saw a ball of fire above Barsauma's head; it remained there for a long time. Jacob was amazed. The day after, he told the brethren who were with him what he had seen.

3 On the morning of that day Barsauma took leave of Jacob and went down to Antioch. All the city came out to welcome him; but he continued down to the harbor, where he embarked on a ship bound for Palestine.

4 After coming ashore, he traveled to Jerusalem incognito, warning his disciples constantly not to reveal his identity to anyone. So he entered the city secretly[112] and took up lodgings in a certain large monastery where he was known.[113]

5 When those monks saw him, they taken by surprise. He raised his hand. "I hope you are not going to tell anyone about me!" he said. "Give me a few days' respite to recover from my journey!" So they kept quiet about it and told no one.

§ 91 *The sixty-first sign. The Jews assemble en masse and meet their deaths.*

1 Now what had happened earlier was this. The priests and the leaders of the Jewish people from the whole land of Galilee and its environs had and gone up to Jerusalem together to present a long

109. Barrington Atlas 67, D-F3, the whole region between the ʿAmūq Valley and the Euphrates.

110. Note the variant reading "resides," which, if correct, implies that Jacob of Cyrrhestica was still alive when this was written. This might explain why the writer seems to assume, in § 90.1, that the reader knows his name.

111. Jacob lived on a hill about 5.5 km from Cyrrhus (Theodoret, *Relig. hist.* 21); cf. Evagrius, *Eccl. hist.* 2.9.

112. Cf. Jn 7:10.

113. This was the monastery of Photina on Mount Sion, as Barsauma's disciples reveal at § 95.4.

petition to the empress Eudocia. They praised her with resounding acclamations: "You are the Mistress of the World and we are the slaves of your Royal Highness. Without you we are unable to live. The emperor Constantine the Great issued a decree forbidding us to enter the district of Jerusalem. Have mercy on your slaves and permit us now to enter the ruins of the temple which Solomon built and pray there!"

2 The empress Eudocia granted the Jews their request, issuing the following decree: "The Jews have the right to enter Jerusalem and pray in the temple that was built by King Solomon."

3 Having obtained this decree from the empress, the Jews leapt for joy. The spirit of arrogance entered them, only to make their shame the greater in the end. They wrote a letter to the Jewish people and sent it to the various provinces of Persia and to all the great cities of the Roman Empire.

4 "To the great and mighty people of the Jews from the priests and leaders of Galilee: warm greetings!" Such was their opening. "We write to inform you that the time of our people's diaspora is past. The day has come for our tribes to be reunited. The Roman emperors have decreed that our city, Jerusalem, is to be restored to us. Make haste, then, and come to Jerusalem for the Feast of Tabernacles! Our kingdom is going to be established in Jerusalem!" There was much more of the same, but this was the gist of their letter.

5 With false hopes raised by this misleading letter a great number of Jews assembled at Jerusalem. Observing the appointed time, they entered the city on the Feast of Tabernacles. Now on the very day when the Jews entered Jerusalem openly for the first time, Barsauma entered the same city in secret.

6 Barsauma entered Jerusalem at noon, hastily left the monastery, and went down discreetly to pray at the Pool of Siloah.[114] Then he went back to the monastery where he was staying.

7 About twenty of his brethren went their separate way up to the ruined temple of Solomon to see the "pinnacle of the temple" where Satan placed our Savior when he tempted him and said: "Throw yourself down from here!"[115]

114. Cf. Neh 3:15; Jn 9.

115. Mt 4:5–7.

8 When Barsauma's disciples looked closely at the ruins of the temple built by Solomon, they saw great numbers of Jews, clothed in black, who wept, shredded their clothing, sprinkled ashes on their heads, and sat down on the ruins of the temple, groaning. It was noon.

9 The Jews who were assembled there numbered about one hundred and three thousand men and women. When the disciples saw them, they were standing right opposite them, in full view.

§ 92 *The sixty-second sign. The Jewish people have a vision.*

1 One of the brethren who were standing there saw all those Jewish people clothed in black and sitting on the ashes of the ruined building and there welled up in his mind a passage from the Prophets. This disciple asked two of his companions: "Which passage from the Prophets do you think is going to come true any moment now?" They said: "We do not know."

2 "There are two predictions in the Prophets," he went on, "which are about to come true. But look out! We must hurry away from here! The Wrath of the Lord is on the point of striking the Jewish people!" "What words are written about this moment?" his companions asked; then he said clearly which passages he meant.[116]

3 Hardly had he finished explaining the words when a sudden great clamor was heard from the Jews. They were screaming in terror and running in all directions. A frightening vision had appeared to them: God's armies were bearing down on them from heaven. The Jews could see this apparition, but the Christians could see nothing. One or two of the disciples did, however, see sand rising up like a cloud and covering the Jews.

4 Many stones were flying through that cloud and raining blows on the Jews. No one could tell where those stones were coming from. All the Jews had cut skins and broken bones. Many of them died there and then, many others a few days later. As for the rest, they were badly wounded. Many were maimed, or lamed.

116. These passages have not yet been identified. Is 31:5, Jer 31:23, and Dn 9:24–27 are potential candidates.

§ 93 *The sixty-third sign. A brother, stoned by the Jews, does not feel the stones hitting him.*

1 The brother who had referred those passages of Scripture to this occasion was mobbed by the Jews, who shouted: "This is the teacher of the Christians. He ought to be stoned!" Then they surrounded him and pelted him with stones. They went on doing this for a long time, but not a stone hit his body, not the slightest scratch did he receive.

2 At the sound of the screaming all Jerusalem came out, from the greatest to the least. The Christians saw the Jews broken, cut, and cast down on the ground. The Jews were ashamed to admit that the blow had fallen squarely from heaven on them. To cover their shame, they were shouting: "Those Christians massacred us."

3 When the soldiers and the clergy (κληρικοί) heard this, they said it was true. Now the empress Eudocia had decreed that no one should harm the Jewish people. The clergy now sought to ingratiate themselves with her by taking sides with the Jews and joined them in trying to catch and arrest Barsauma's disciples. The brethren landed plenty of blows on the clergy and the soldiers.

4 The soldiers, the clergy, and the Jews acted together. Their next step was to cut themselves branches from the olive-trees and surround the palace of the empress in Bethlehem, about six miles away from Jerusalem. They began to salute her with their olive-branches, adding: "Some ruffians have come from Mesopotamia wearing the respectable habit (σχῆμα) of monks. They have provoked a great conflict in the city and have ruined it. It is plain to see that many people have been killed. They are lying in the streets. The courtyards and the cisterns are filled with the corpses of the massacred."

5 When the empress Eudocia heard this, she was extremely worried. She could see great bruises on the clergy and the soldiers. Thinking their version of events was true, she shuddered with fear and sent in the army to seize the murderers.

6 As for the disciples of Barsauma, when they saw that the Roman army had come out against them, they began to say among themselves: "This means we are all going to die. Let us at least keep it a secret that we are the disciples of Barsauma! Otherwise, many will turn against him, as our leader. After all, we are going to be put to death today as murderers!"

7 The soldiers and the cathedral clergy arrested eighteen of the brethren. They rained harsh blows on them, insulting them with the vilest of names and spitting in their faces. As for the brethren, they rejoiced and exulted. This made the soldiers and the clergy, who thought they were really murderers, grind their teeth in fury.

8 Then one of the brethren climbed up and stood on top of a boulder. He made a gesture to the people to be quiet and began to speak in a loud voice: "We do not despise you, as you think; nor is it because we are murderers that we are laughing. It is just that we are filled with joy to think where it is that God considers us worthy to die. Our fathers' bones will exult in their graves. Christ has given us sinners the privilege of being put to death in Jerusalem. In Jerusalem, where prophets and apostles have been massacred. In Jerusalem, where Christ Himself was crucified. Now that we, too, are going to die in Jerusalem, innocent of any crime, we should indeed be glad.

9 "But you, who are killing us for nothing, must prepare yourselves for the weeping and the gnashing of teeth which is kept in store for your brothers, the Jews. Your friends, the crucifiers. This is because you have joined forces with that abominable party to kill those who worship the Crucified. We have a true hope in the Crucified, whom we have come here to worship, that He will show you signs and wonders and that you will be put to shame."

10 At this the soldiers and the clergy dragged that brother violently off the boulder, forced him to the ground, insulted and beat him. Then they took the brethren and locked them up alive in the military prison (Syriac: *beth signas*, from τὰ σίγνα).[117]

11 The empress decreed that a judge should hear the brethren the following day and put them to death. In the morning, the Jews brought the corpses of their dead and piled them up at the door of the prison. Then the empress gave orders that her most trusted officials (Syriac: *šarrīrē*) and the priests (Syriac: *qaššīšē*) of the cathedral were to go and inspect the corpses.

12 The orders she gave were as follows: "If the Jews were killed with sticks, let sticks be used to kill their murderers! If their corpses

117. Originally the shrine in a legionary camp, where the standards were kept under lock and key.

bear the marks of stoning, let those who stoned them die in the same way! If it was knives and swords that killed them, let their killers' bodies be cut into pieces with knives and swords!"[118]

13 When the imperial officials and the cathedral priests arrived, they had the corpses stripped. But they could not see a single bruise from a stick on them, nor any injury caused by a stone, nor any wound inflicted with iron. There was not a cut on their skins, not a broken bone in their bodies.

§ 94 *The sixty-fourth sign. A Jewish woman shrivels up.*

1 All of a sudden, while they were inspecting those corpses, a Jewish woman fell down beside these and died in front of their eyes. Immediately she shriveled up and became like a piece of dry wood. The imperial officials saw her and were mightily afraid. One of them said to his companions: "These corpses may all have been killed by the monks; but who killed the woman who died just now in front of our eyes?"

2 The imperial officials proclaimed: "Let the Jewish priests (Syriac: *kohnē*) be seized and handcuffed until they reveal who slaughtered these corpses!" Then the soldiers began to carry out these orders.

3 Suddenly, however, the Jewish priests shouted: "We beg of your authority, do not let us perish because of those righteous men who have been imprisoned! Release them and let them go in peace! We have sinned against God. It is God's wrath that has killed us.

4 "We were sitting on the ashes of the temple and grieving, watched by those Christians, when we saw, all at once, a great host of angels bearing shining spears. The next thing we saw was a great army of soldiers coming against us from the direction of those Christians, their drawn swords flashing like lightning.

5 "In our terror we screamed out loud and fell down, bowled over by fear. All these corpses which are lying in front of you died of sheer terror. We were ashamed to admit God's wrath was the cause of our death, so we accused those righteous men of a crime. They have committed no sin."

6 "Who can bear witness to this?" asked the imperial officials. "The corpses themselves," said the Jewish priests. "Those who lost their lives bear witness. Their bodies display no wound inflicted by

118. Cf. Ex 21:24; Lv 24:20.

steel, no injury caused by a stone. Had they been killed by these Christians, the blows of stones and steel would have left their marks. As for the fact that we saw the hosts of angels, all our people can bear witness to that."

7 This statement was supported by all the Jewish people. "The testimony of our priests is true," they said. "Release the righteous men who have been imprisoned and let them go in peace! We do not want all our people to perish because of them!" Having seen that woman's sudden death, they were mortally afraid. They thought that they would all die as she had done, shriveling up like a piece of dry wood. That is why they shouted out: "Release the righteous men and let them go in peace! We do not want all our people to perish because of them!"

8 The imperial officials, the clergy, and the soldiers were all afraid. The Christian people were also troubled. They had not realized before that a blow from God had wrought havoc among the Jews.

9 As for the imperial officials, when they heard and saw what had happened, they reported swiftly to their mistress, the empress Eudocia, who groaned and was mortally afraid. She sent a petition to the brethren who were in prison, with the following entreaty: "Forgive me this offense! I was unaware of it. Many led me astray. I thought you had brought conflict to our city by massacring the Jews. But now God has brought the truth to light. Your innocence is proven."

§ 95 *The sixty-fifth sign. Five Jewish men shrivel up.*

1 After this the empress ordered that the corpses be buried, and some Jews lifted up their dead to take them out of the city. The entire Christian community went out with the Jews to watch.

2 Now certain Christians began to say to one another: "Perhaps it was out of fear that the Jews said they had seen hosts of angels." At that moment five of the Jewish corpse-bearers fell down dead, their bodies as hard as stones. This convinced the entire Christian community. Now everyone acknowledged that the blow which had fallen on the Jews had come from God.

3 The officials reported this event also to their mistress, the empress, at which she became so much afraid that she fell into a dead faint. She sent an abject entreaty to those brethren who were in prison. The imperial officials opened the door of the military prison, went in, and prostrated themselves in front of the brethren, the tears streaming

down their cheeks. The brethren were aware of none of the things which had happened, so the officials and the clergy told them all that God had done to the Jews, and invited them to take some food and drink some water.

4 Once the brethren realized that they were not going to be executed, they told the imperial officials and the cathedral priests about their master: "We are the slaves of a certain righteous man. Our master is here in Jerusalem with us. We cannot eat or drink without his permission." "Who is your master," they asked, "and where is he?" "Our master," the brethren answered, "is Barsauma. He lodges at the monastery of Photina of Sion."[119]

5 Now when they learned that they were Barsauma's disciples and that he was there in the city, a great confusion fell on them and they began to raise a great clamor. Then the entire Christian people, from the greatest to the least, began to run to the place where Barsauma was and prostrated themselves at his feet, weeping and groaning.

6 This, too, was reported to the empress Eudocia, who shuddered with the greatest possible trepidation and, deeply ashamed, sent an urgent plea to Barsauma: "You know, sir, how the Jewish people oppress and persecute the Christians, so I entreat your holy person not to harbor resentment toward me. The governor (ἡγεμών) will come and, by lawful means, release your disciples from the military prison in which they are being held. In the eyes of justice, your disciples are not guilty. But in order to prevent the Jews from slandering me and saying that I have acted out of regard for your person, I want them to be released by the intervention of a judge."

7 The empress sent to the governor at Caesarea-on-Sea to come and release those brethren from prison. Between the messenger's departure and the governor's arrival six full days went by.

8 Now many bishops happened to be present in Jerusalem at that time. When these heard the empress's words, they thought her inten-

119. Józef T. Milik, "La topographie de Jérusalem vers la fin de l'époque byzantine," *Mélanges de l'Université Saint Joseph* 37 (1960–61): 164–67, locates this monastery next to the church of the nameless Samaritan woman of Jn 4:1–30, whose name, as tradition claimed to know, was "Saint Photina the Samaritan" (Ernest Honigmann, *Le couvent de Barsauma et le patriarcat jacobite d'Antioche et de Syrie*, CSCO 146, Subsidia 7 [Louvain: Imprimerie Orientaliste L. Durbecq, 1954], 17).

tion was to help the Jews. So the rumor spread among the Christians that the empress intended to kill the brethren in some underhand manner. People began to say: "Let us set fire to the empress and to all her entourage!"

9 Then the bishops wrote a binding letter to all cities and their regions, summoning the masses to show their support for the brethren. So the masses flocked to Jerusalem, which was filled to the limit; indeed, the city could not hold the great number which gathered. They were waiting to see what decree the empress would issue in the end; then they were going to burn her with fire.

10 Six days went by, and the governor came with a great retinue. He kept his distance from Jerusalem, fearing to enter the city, in case they should stone him. He sent the following message to the brethren in prison: "I am a Christian and a slave and worshipper of all Christians. I beg you on my bended knee, let your word rule the masses! Tell them not to stone me for your sake! Then I will be able to come in and visit you with peaceful intentions, to receive your blessing and to deal with your case, that you may be released with honor and great rejoicing."

11 The brethren were still on their guard against the governor, in case he was coming with treacherous intent. So they sent word to him: "If you come as a man of peace, we, too, are men of peace. But if you come with treacherous intent, beware! We are armed with the power of Christ. Whatever your intention, we shall receive you in the same spirit."

12 Then the brethren sent out heralds throughout the city and its outskirts to make the following public announcement: "The righteous men who are in prison have given this order. Let no one prevent the governor from coming in!"

13 Just then Barsauma joined his disciples in their prison. They welcomed him with mixed feelings. They were happy to see their hero, of course; but they wept, too, because they were in prison.

§ 96 *The sixty-sixth sign. An earthquake in Jerusalem.*

1 Then the governor entered the place where they were. He stood there in front of them, shaking with fear, and said: "I have not come to judge you. Your case has been judged by God and He has resolved it. I have come by imperial decree to represent the secular law. I do not want to hear many words, only the cause of the incident. Let the eldest

among you tell me in no more than ten sentences how it all began. Innumerable people are assembled, waiting to hear your defense."

2 It was Barsauma who opened his mouth to give the judge his answer. But with the second word which came from his lips, a violent earthquake started. From the belly of the earth was heard something like the sound of loud thunder. There arose a cacophony in which the sounds of wood creaking, stones grinding, and people groaning were mixed together. The next moment a huge roar emerged from the bellies of the people. The ceilings of buildings were being lifted right off their walls, and all the columns were knocking into one another.

3 As for the judge, he was lying prostrate at Barsauma's feet, on the point of dying of fear, and others fell—shouting, trembling, weeping—on top of him.

4 Then the earthquake subsided. The buildings stood firm. By the will of God, each and every one of the columns which had been knocking into one another was established on its own base. In the earthquake which shook Jerusalem, violent as it had been, not a single person died, nor did the buildings of the city collapse. Evidently, the grace of God prevented the city from collapsing, so that the Christians might have no trouble because of Barsauma.

5 Meanwhile, Barsauma grasped the governor's hand and, after a considerable struggle, raised him up. Then, holding him by the arms, he said: "Have no fear! You are not going to die."

6 Mustering his courage, the man recovered his strength, stood up, and ordered the heralds to proclaim: "The Crucified has overcome." Hereupon the entire people without exception, both outside and within, began to cry out: "The Crucified has overcome." The voice of the people continued to thunder, gaining in strength, for a long time, like the din of a storm at sea, and the city's buildings were shaken again by the prodigious noise of that shouting.

7 At this point Barsauma, in the company of the governor, came out onto the street. The governor urged him to intone the response to the first psalm of the office, but Barsauma delegated this task to one of his disciples.

8 Now that disciple had his eye on the Jews, who were trembling. He glimpsed Samaritans, who were becoming agitated and making as if to escape. He looked at the pagans, who were hanging their heads in order to hide their faces. The Christians, by contrast, were filled with

exultation. Inspired by what he saw, he composed a response and intoned the psalm in a loud voice.

Behold, the Jews are ashamed; the Samaritans sit and mourn.
The pagans bow down their heads; the Church exults in the Cross.

9 This was the psalm he intoned.

Let God arise and let all his enemies be scattered!
Let those who hate him make their escape from his presence![120]

With a powerful massed voice, the crowds repeated the response after the disciple. As for the Jews, the Samaritans, and the pagans, they began to distance themselves from the Christians, running in all directions.

10 Meanwhile, the Christian people praised God with the voice of thanksgiving. They constituted choirs, each race singing in its own tongue: Romans, Syrians, Greeks, Persians, Palestinians, and Egyptians. Many peoples' praises were mingled there. It was like the roar of a storm-wind above the clash of the ocean-waves. On the governor's instructions the choirs involved in chanting that office were counted and found to be five hundred in number. All the monks of the wilderness and all the people from the villages and the cities were there.

11 Surrounded by the choir of his brethren, Barsauma processed through the city. Many poured out fine wines and select oils on the ground in front of him, scattered expensive spices in his direction as he walked, or sprinkled him with expensive perfumes. They escorted Barsauma to the great church which had been constructed on Mount Sion, and he offered up the oblation there.[121]

12 A full account in writing of the events occasioned by Barsauma was sent by the judge to the emperor Theodosius and to the greater cities. Everyone who heard it read out glorified God, to whom indeed praise, honor, and thanks are due, forever and ever, Amen!

13 Now the empress Eudocia was much alarmed. She urged Barsauma with many tears and spoke to him as follows: "Sir, I am your servant. All my possessions are at your disposal."

14 "Far be it from me," said Barsauma in answer, "that I should leave the Door of God, at which I stand, and stand at the door of human beings, who are beneath me. For God's Door, at which we

120. Ps 68:1.

121. This was presumably the Hagia Sion church, in the southwest corner of the city.

stand, opens swiftly whenever we choose to knock; and once we have entered there, we find there everything we love. When we are in need, He gladly gives whatever we ask for.

15 "But your door does not open for us every time we knock, nor do the doors of other human beings; and once we have entered through your doorway, we do not find in your house everything we love. When we are in need, you do not give us whatever we ask for.

16 "Therefore we will not leave the Great Door at which we stand and knock at your door. We shall take everything that we need from the Great Door at which we stand. We have no need of any human's door."

17 After this the empress bowed down low at his feet, and he departed in peace.

18 On the morning of the following day, when Barsauma prepared to leave Jerusalem, a great number of Christians gathered at the place where he was staying. From the morning until the evening Barsauma continued to teach them the word of God.

19 Many people of other religions came, too, though without being open about their religion. When they heard his teaching on faith, each and every one of them began to weep for himself. Many of them, convinced by his teaching, became believers.

20 At sunset, Barsauma left Jerusalem and set out for the East. The entire population of the city saw him off with censers and incense, candles and lamps. The greatest and the least were united in their grief. Barsauma prayed over them, blessed them, and sent them off, back to the city. His sea-voyage was serene.

§ 97 *Many signs which are not written in this book.*

1 The last part of the way he covered on foot, and all the cities and villages came out to meet him with their bishops, their monks, and the administrators of their provinces. He performed many signs in a number of different places, while he was traveling along that way, and halted many diseases fatal to man or beast. At last, serene, he arrived back inside his monastery.

§ 98 *The sixty-seventh sign. A village, cursed by him, is swept away by the Euphrates.*

1 A great dispute arose between two large towns on the river Euphrates. When both parties went to Barsauma's place to pray, he

spoke to those who were in the wrong: "My sons, do not upset your brothers! Make peace with them! We are all going to die and return to the dust from which we came. Let us not burden ourselves with sins deserving of eternal damnation for the sake of this soil from which we were created!"

2 But those people, thinking he was taking sides with their neighbors, answered with one voice: "We came to you for prayer, not for judgment. You have not been set up as judge over us. Let this matter be our concern!"

3 "I may not be your judge," he persisted, "but I wish you peace and tranquility. However, since you reject love and peace, listen and I will tell you my judgment. Whether these brothers of yours have wrongfully encroached on your territory, or you on theirs, that town which is the cause of offense to its neighbors will become the riverbed. The Lord will see to it."

4 Not long after that, God commanded the Euphrates to leave its original course. It flowed straight toward the town of those wrongdoers, sweeping its houses away, overthrowing its monuments, dragging away its wood, carrying its stones a great way off, destroying its beautiful vineyards, pulling up its fine vegetable-gardens, washing away the earth from its good lands, and uprooting its delightful plantations. It became a stretch of rocky rapids in the course of the Euphrates. Thus Barsauma's curse was fulfilled.

§ 99 *The sixty-eighth sign. The two bows of many colors.*

1 One day, around the same time, while Barsauma was at his monastery, he saw two small bows back-to-back, colored like those which appear in the clouds on a rainy day. "What is the rainbow-colored sign over there?" he asked his brethren. They did not know what to say.

2 At the time, they did not understand the hidden meaning of what had happened. But when Barsauma came into protracted conflict with perverse heresies, his disciples understood that those variegated bows had been a sign from God that he would overcome.

3 God gave Noah the bow in the clouds as a sign of victory, that he might make war on Satan, who had overpowered that ruinous generation, causing them to be overwhelmed by the waters of the Flood.[122]

122. Gn 6:11f.; 9:8–17.

4 In the same way He gave the two bows of victory to Barsauma, that he might take the two covenants of the Scriptures in his right hand and in his left and make war on the party of the apostates (Syriac: *kōfūrē*),[123] whom Satan has killed by the urge to investigate. Paul said something similar with reference to the cross.[124]

§ 100 *The sixty-ninth sign. Water is turned into milk.*

1 At another time the water and oil in a lamp were turned into milk in Barsauma's presence. This happened at dawn after an all-night vigil.

§ 101 *The seventieth sign. A sweet smell fills the air, and an angel appears.*

1 The following day was a Sunday. Barsauma was standing outside the window of the building and singing in antiphony with his disciples when a smell of incense unlike any other filled the air and the angel of the Lord suddenly appeared, standing between the two choirs of the brethren while they performed the service. His appearance was that of an old man clothed in white. Now this fragrance was often to be smelt where Barsauma was.

§ 102 *Many signs which have not been written down.*

1 Other signs also appeared in the place where he used to pray. But the signs which God performed where he was are so many in number that I have left them out, because of my inadequacy. I now come, therefore, to the end of his contest (ἀγών), the last part of the tale of his victorious deeds.

§ 103 *The death of Zachariah, alias Zuṭo the Mountaineer, the bishop of Samosata.*

1 Barsauma had now got the better of his enemy in the fight and was on the way to winning the crown of a champion (ἀθλητής). Satan had been exposed by trials of his own design. At this juncture, the zenith of the holy man's fortunes and the nadir of the opposing party's,

123. The majority of bishops at Chalcedon overturned the synod of 449, which had opposed Dyophysitism, and so were described as apostates by the party to which Barsauma belonged.

124. 2 Cor 6:7; cf. 2 Cor 6:2–10.

Zachariah, Barsauma's fellow student—called "Zuṭo the Mountaineer" among the brethren—became bishop of Samosata.[125]

2 Motivated by envy of his righteousness, wicked men stirred up a conspiracy against this bishop and bribed some of the soldiers of the city to stone him in the street. When the stoning began, he stretched his hands toward heaven and said to his fellow bishops: "Leave me, everyone! I intend to die alone!" Then he went to sleep in peace, surrendered his spirit to Christ, and was buried.

3 Because of this stoning, Barsauma went up to Constantinople and obtained an audience with the emperor Theodosius.

§ 104 The emperor Theodosius grants him an audience.

1 Such was the joy of the emperor at seeing Barsauma that he embraced and kissed him. "Sir," he said, "I have wanted to see you for a long time. I would have summoned you here to pray in our country and bless our City and its inhabitants, had I not been reluctant to burden you with a tiring journey. Now that God has brought you here, I will gladly do everything you ask. Your word is my command."

2 Then the emperor urged him to accept great gifts from him, but he declined them. Realising that the holy man might be unwilling to accept secular objects, he had had vessels made for the altar of sacrifice. There were golden chalices and pyxes set with pearls and precious stones, including some very valuable gems. These choice vessels, together with veils of silk and purple of the finest quality, the emperor offered to Barsauma. 'Sir,' he said, 'here is a small blessing. Your servant offers it to you for God's altar. I beg you, as your son, to accept it gladly. May it be used in your monastery for the worship of God!'

3 Now the most negligible object there was a small veil. This Barsauma accepted with the following words: "I should not like you to think that I have rejected your offering, so I have taken this, as the 'firstfruits of the harvest'; I pray that your offering may be accepted in heaven as here on earth! These magnificent vessels are not suitable for monks. Such things are only required by the finest of churches in the greatest of cities."

4 When the emperor found him adamant in refusal, he was very much in awe of him. Barsauma rose in his esteem to the status of one

125. Cf. § 12.

of the apostles. "Now, indeed," he said, "I can believe all the great things I have heard about you. It is not just because you refuse my gifts that I believe. I am amazed at the perfection of your mind."

5 As for Barsauma, he spoke with the emperor about the true Faith and a god-fearing way of life. The emperor congratulated him on his piety. He and his courtiers expressed their admiration for the holy man and praised God for endowing the Christians with such wisdom.

§ 105 *Theodosius urges him to be a father to all the bishops.*

1 After this the emperor urged him to accept the office of archbishop of the great city of Antioch, teaching everyone the true Way[126] and appointing his disciples to the other episcopal sees.[127]

2 This was Barsauma's reply: "An eagle's element is air. It would drown if it exchanged this for the water of the sea, just as a fish, which has always lived in water, would die in the air. It is the same with a person who was reared on the open pastures. He cannot live in the midst of cultivated land. He thrives on the open pastures, as an eagle on the air. Conversely, the open pastures are difficult for a human being who has been reared on cultivated land, because he cannot endure the hardships of the wilderness."

3 Then the emperor urged Barsauma to take care of the management of the Church and of the poor, even while remaining in the habit of a mourner, and to be a director for the bishops in the cities and for the judges in all regions.

4 The emperor took his own ring and gave it to Barsauma. "This ring which I give you now, sir," he said, "is my own seal. When you write me a letter, seal it with my ring. By this I shall know it is from you!" In all simplicity of heart, Barsauma accepted the ring. The emperor did not explain that by giving it to him he was investing him with his own authority.

126. Acts 9:2; cf. Acts 11:26.

127. If this is true, it means that Theodosius II was already looking for a successor to Domnus of Antioch some months before the latter was deposed by the Second Council of Ephesus (August 449).

§ 106 *The emperor writes a letter to the synod.*

1 Later, the emperor wrote a letter and sent copies to the whole empire of the Romans, summoning all the bishops to Ephesus in Asia.[128]

2 The emperor Theodosius wrote another decree, which he sent to all the bishops when they had assembled, as follows:[129] "Theodosius and Valentinian, the Christian emperors, to all the true bishops of the Catholic Church, warm greetings! I inform the holy synod of the priests of God that Barsauma, the monastic leader, has been chosen by God. You know, better than we do, that he is true in his faith and respectable in his orthodoxy; perfect in his good deeds and complete in the fear of God; luminous in knowledge and excellent in wisdom; full of zeal and complete in love; pure from corruption and free from the respect of persons; unsoiled by the love of mammon; a lover of mankind, and a servant of God, trusted by Christ with the stewardship of the apostles. What is more, great signs like those of the apostles are performed through his agency.

3 "Moreover, I have tested him in many ways and have found him to be flawless. I begged him to become the next archbishop of Antioch, but he has declined. I offered him great gifts, and he has refused them. At last I have persuaded him to become father and director to me, while remaining in the habit of a mourner, and to have the bishops and judges of my entire dominion at his command. Let the judgment of the synod of bishops be decided according to the word of that Slave of God!

4 "You should all be aware that I have given him my own ring, as father and director of the entire empire of the Romans, set in authority over all our people, an authority exceeding that of Joseph over the land of Egypt,[130] that is to say, equal to my own and to that of the episcopal see of Antioch. Let the archimandrite Barsauma be a hearer at the synod of all the bishops!"

5 When the decree of the emperor had been read out within the synod of all the bishops, they all went out to greet Barsauma and welcome him with great gladness.

128. Barrington Atlas 1, I3; Michael, *Chron.* 8.6 and 7; cf. Gregory, *Chron. eccl.* 1.161–64. See also the anonymous Syriac *Chron. 846*, ed. 212; tr. 162.

129. This differs considerably from the letters preserved in *ACC* I.47–48, 108–9.

130. Cf. Gn 41:37–45.

§ 107 *The synod of Ephesus.*

1 So a great and powerful synod sat down in the holy church of the city of Ephesus. Barsauma, however, was not in the habit of sitting down, so the bishops placed a lectern at the head of the synod. In front of him, on this lectern, they laid the Gospel, resting on a cushion. Some of them even took up this Gospel and lifted it up to lower it onto his crown, so that he might be ordained a bishop by that same synod; but Barsauma declined the honor.

2 Every word uttered at that synod of bishops was spoken at Barsauma's behest. Bishop Dioscoros of Alexandria the Great and the bishop of Jerusalem, it is true, argued the need for certain ecclesiastical canons, but it was Barsauma who directed the whole performance.

3 After the synod had been dismissed and everyone had returned in peace to his country and his city, the emperor Theodosius wrote to Barsauma, summoning him to Constantinople. When he arrived, the emperor so rejoiced in his presence that he kept him with him for a few days, before letting him go down to Antioch to convene another synod of bishops there to appoint a (new) bishop for that city.[131]

§ 108 *Theodosius writes an open letter about him.*

1 While Barsauma set out by sea for Antioch, Theodosius wrote a letter (σάκρα) and sent it with his officials overland. It was received in the city of Antioch and in all the great cities.

2 It read as follows: "Theodosius and Valentinian, the Christian emperors, to the whole Roman Empire, much peace! All you who are under the authority of our Majesty must know that we have asked Barsauma, the Slave of Christ, to help us bear the weight of government in this time of confusion and of disturbance.

3 "It will be his responsibility to take care of the churches of Christ and to be both teacher of the Orthodox Faith and commander of the judges in every province! He shall see to it that judgment is given to the poor without corruption! Let him be father to the bishops of the churches and executive (Syriac: *mdabbrono*) of our Majesty's imperial authority!

131. Domnus of Antioch was deposed by the Second Synod of Ephesus during its final session.

4 "Moreover, we decree that he be placed in authority over the bishops and the judges of our empire, to create and to abrogate, to establish and to overthrow. If any dare oppose him, he shall be punishable under the law. All who oppose Barsauma are opposed to God, because he is His own trusted Slave.[132] If God does this righteous man's will, how much more do we, being sinners, owe him obedience and assent; and if God is not against him, how much less should we, being weak, resist him?"

5 When this imperial letter was read out in the great cities, many hurried to see Barsauma. Their first goal was to obtain his blessing, their second, to solve all kinds of problems. All those who were suffering from pains and diseases came to Christ's champion (ἀθλητής), and he healed their cruel pains by the power of our Redeemer and drove out many evil spirits.

6 All those who were oppressed and coerced by violence flocked to him from all countries; and each man's case was judged with rectitude, with neither bribery, nor the iniquitous respect of persons. The poor and the oppressed rejoiced in his greatness, while plunderers and the grasping could only grind their teeth. The wicked were all struck down by him, while the righteous prospered by his elevation.[133] In short, the party of the apostates was put to shame by his faith, whereas the side of the true rejoiced in that upright man's teaching. Every day God in heaven was praised on his account, while his prayers brought about Satan's humiliation everywhere.

§ 109 The seventy-first sign. A general, cursed by him, breaks his bones in a fall and dies.

1 So after Satan had seen that Barsauma had driven him out of many countries, he entered, envious and deceitful, the minds of the clergy (κληρικοί) of Antioch. They paid a great bribe to a certain man, a pagan and a rebel, who was the general (στρατηλάτης) and resided there at that time.[134] Those unprincipled men persuaded this rebel to make a stand against Barsauma.

132. Cf. Heb 3:5.

133. Cf. Ps 72:4.

134. Antioch was the residence of the *magister militum per Orientem* (στρατηλάτης τῆς ἕω).

2 That is how this pagan came to take it into his head to rebel against the emperor Theodosius also. He had the purple clothes and the crown of an emperor all ready for the moment when he would be clothed in majesty at Antioch.[135]

3 Barsauma cursed him: "As our Redeemer, the Christ whom I worship, is true to me, that rebel will fall and suffer two breakages." A few days later, that pagan fell from his horse and broke his leg, dying shortly afterward. In this way Barsauma's prediction that he would suffer "two breakages" came true. The second "breakage" was his death.

§ 110 *The seventy-second sign. The sign is seen concerning his stoning.*

1 Around this time, Barsauma was standing near one of his disciples, and this man was looking at his head, when he had a vision of many people pelting Barsauma with rocks. It appeared to that disciple that a white stone, like a pebble from a river, coming from those people, struck him above his left eye and gave off a report. The disciple who saw this took hold of Barsauma by the head, kissed him on the place where the stone had struck him in his vision, and began to weep.

2 Barsauma was astonished and asked him: "What is this that you have done?" "I saw something miraculous," he replied, "but I cannot explain it to you now." This vision revealed what was going to happen to Barsauma later. From that time onward, that disciple was always thinking about this in private and wondering greatly at it.

3 The following day Barsauma arrived at a large and prosperous city, and all the people there came out to greet him. The judges and the

135. Honigmann (*Le couvent de Barsauma*, 20), citing François Nau ("Deux épisodes de l'histoire juive sous Théodose II [423 et 438] d'après la Vie de Barṣauma le Syrien," *Revue des études juives* 93 [1927]: 202), identifies this man with Zeno (cf. John R. Martindale, ed., *Prosopography of the Later Roman Empire*, vol. 2 of 3 [4], *A.D. 395–527* [Cambridge: Cambridge University Press, 1980], Zeno 6:1199f.), who was thought capable of revolt over the peace terms agreed with Attila in 450, though he is attested as Patricius in October 451 (*ACC* XIX.7 = *ACO* II.1.3, 1057 [Greek; no Latin version is extant]), so the words "A few days later" are disingenuous. Damascius knew a rumor that "the great general of the East," an unnamed pagan, had died after breaking his leg in a fall from a horse and was thereby prevented from killing an emperor (summed up by Photius, *Bibl.* 1301 C).

leading men prostrated themselves before him. When he saw this and heard the uproar of the agitated multitude, he was deeply shaken, groaned bitterly, and shed copious tears.

4 Then he addressed his disciples: "If God does not want my avoidance of occasions of stumbling (lit. "my stumblings") to be wiped out in his sight; and if Christ knows that my soul's agonies will not be cheated of their reward, He will give me a sign of peace in my lifetime, and my eyes will see many people stoning me for the sake of the Crucified. Only then will I be able to believe firmly that the reward of all my hardship is treasured up in his presence."

5 Now when the disciple who, the day before, had had the vision of his stoning heard him asking to be pelted with rocks, he groaned inwardly. Then he knew in his bones that what he had seen would come to pass.

6 Then, weeping, he spoke out loud: "Why have you made this request, master, which will ruin many people? Only if paganism is reestablished in the world can this happen to you. Our Lord grants you everything you ask. We know that. So why have you asked Him for something which may give joy to you, but will kill many? I have believed for some time that this will come to pass in truth; but woe to the whole world . . . !"

7 "Do you not know, my son," Barsauma answered, "the pains which afflict me from within? When I saw emperors and empresses lying on the floor at my feet, I groaned and thought to myself, 'It is in vain that my Lord has so often set me free from the stumbling of my feet.' Whenever I see multitudes doing worship in my presence, and watch judges bent double at my feet, I groan and my limbs shake. Secretly, I am tormented by the thought that this very glory will deprive me of the reward of all my hardship.

8 "The prophets were persecuted, but I am respected; the apostles underwent stoning, but I receive congratulations; the martyrs were slaughtered, whereas I have been elevated; the confessors were reviled, whereas I am praised; and on the cross our Lord was insulted by sinners and weak men, whereas I, a weak man and a sinner, am carried aloft in procession by all the world.

9 "Our Redeemer said—and He tells the truth—'It is enough for the servant to be like his lord, and for the disciple to be like his

master.'[136] So if I were really the Slave of Christ, what was done to his slaves and to Him would have been done to me.

10 "At the end our Lord may well say to me: 'What fine deeds you have done in my service! Instead of doing your duty, which was to worship me, you brought emperors to your feet, though it was no part of their duty to worship you. Instead of doing what they ought, which was to praise me as their Lord, even judges and lords have praised you. Instead of doing what is right, which is to love me, the whole world loves you more than is right. You may have left your family home for my sake, but now both rich and poor offer you their houses. You may have served me as a slave his master, but now both slave and free are at your service.'

11 "I am very much afraid of that utterance of our Lord: 'Many will say to me on that day: "Lord, Lord, open up for us! After all, it was in your Name that we ate and drank. It was in your Name that we prophesied. It was in your Name that we performed miracles. It was in your Name that we drove out demons."' But He will answer: 'I do not know you.'[137]

12 "Another thing our Lord said in his Gospel-teaching frightens me, too: 'You will come to a bad end, scribes and Pharisees, for your hypocrisy! You appear to the world as righteous men, but inside you are full of greed and evil.'[138] 'You resemble whitewashed sepulchres, white on the outside, on the inside full only of filth!'[139] 'You will come to a bad end, scribes and Pharisees, for your hypocrisy! You swallow up the homes of widows on the pretext of lengthening your prayers! Your punishment will be the greater for it.'[140]

13 "It comes down to this, my children.[141] Those who herd swine in humble obscurity have the better part."[142]

14 He was evidently distressed, and all his disciples, hearing, felt the same distress and began to weep downheartedly.

136. Mt 10:25.

137. Mt 7:22f., amplified.

138. Cf. Mt 23:29.

139. Mt 23:27.

140. Mt 23:14; Mk 12:40; Lk 20:47.

141. Something apparently alluding to 2 Cor 1:18 has been omitted here. The transmitted text makes no sense.

142. Cf. Lk 15:11–32.

15 As for Barsauma, he made up his mind to go down and visit the king of Persia. He planned to demolish the temple of the fire which he worships, insult his Majesty, strike the Magians, revile the pagans, and so provoke him to have him killed.

16 Now Barsauma had gone down to Persia on an earlier occasion with the same idea. He had actually reviled the Magians and struck the pagans, but no one had laid a finger on him. Fear and trembling had fallen on them. Everyone had been afraid to speak in his presence.

§ 111 *Certain unprincipled men write a false report on him.*

1 Now he frustrated certain unprincipled men who lived at that time and they drew up the following false report and sent it to the emperor Theodosius.

2 "This criminal impostor Barsauma, to whom Your Majesty has entrusted the entire Roman Empire, eats and drinks great quantities of meat and wine and has his hair cut in the style of a cleric. His head may be covered with the great habit (σχῆμα) of a mourner, but he is a hypocrite.

3 "He claims that he does not sit down, while in fact he lies on soft cloth all night long. He claims not to accept gold from anyone, while in fact the silver and gold taken by the judges in bribes and seized from the poor fills many storehouses, and all of these belong to him."

4 When this wicked report was presented to the emperor, he was astonished at their audacity and shocked by the injustice of their words; for he realized that it was a false accusation.

§ 112 *Barsauma goes up to Constantinople a second time.*

1 Now Barsauma had certain friends who were great men in the empire. These men sent urgently to him in the East, telling him to come with all haste to Constantinople, because of the report which had been published. When Barsauma received this letter from his friends, he promptly went up to the Imperial City and obtained an audience with the emperor Theodosius.

2 When the emperor saw him, he was so glad that he ran to meet him and embraced and kissed him. In doing so, he laid his hand on his

hair and, feeling it, laughed with delight. "Dirty liars!" he shouted. "Curse all oppressors and slanderers! Shame on those who accuse such a true man!"

3 Then the emperor addressed his slaves: "Those liars wrote in their report that the hair of Barsauma's head had been cut. But we can see with our own eyes that it is twisted into plaits of three strands[143] from his head right down to his heels. Who would believe slander, rather than the evidence of his own eyesight?"

§ 113 The second imperial letter and the death of Theodosius.

1 The emperor sat down again and wrote a second letter (σάκρα), more important than the first, with a view to sending it to every district. It was about piety, Barsauma, and the true Faith in Christ.

2 Now the good times and the bad times are determined from the beginning. Each of them will be fulfilled at the date which has been assigned to it. Night succeeds day at the appointed hour, and winter follows summer in due season. In the same way, times of rejoicing and of peace are followed by times of hardship and chastisement. All times are destined to give way to others. Accordingly, the emperor Theodosius died at a time of peace, because a time of hardship was due to begin very soon. But woe to him who brings on the evil![144] Good will come again, according to Scripture, and blessed is he who brings it on!

3 So it was with Josiah, king of Judah, who was more zealous for the Faith than any other king. At a time when he was filled with zeal and faith, God said to him, "You have fulfilled my Will in every respect and have given satisfaction in my sight. I have loved you as I did your father, David.

4 "It is not that I have despised you, or that I have rejected your prayer. But I see that the time for the chastisement of my people Israel is approaching fast. For this reason I am gathering you to your fathers in peace, so that you will not see the evil which I am going to bring

143. The MSS read "doubled on three times," probably a corruption occasioned by the rarity of the Syriac words originally used here for "twisted into plaits" and "strands."

144. Cf. Mt 26:24.

upon my people Israel."[145] So Josiah was gathered to his family, and only then did evil come upon the sons of Israel.

§ 114 *The reign of Marcian.*

1 In the days of the emperor Theodosius utter peace had reigned in the churches of Christ, but now the "time of trial" was due to begin. This was why Theodosius died at this juncture, while Faith still reigned on earth. His successor was Marcian, under whom it was revealed what was meant by "the time of trial" of which all the prophets speak.

2 For not one of the true Scriptures is devoid of evidence concerning this; and I wish I could comment on them all and demonstrate the relevance of certain passages to the present "time of trial." But I have no leisure for that. I must press on toward the conclusion of Barsauma's story.

3 Now the emperor Marcian adopted the policy of establishing that heresy which was originally called after Simon the Magician, then after Paul of Samosata, the bishop of Antioch, and, later still, after Nestorius, bishop of the Imperial City in the days of the emperor Theodosius.[146]

4 Because of this heresy Nestorius was anathematized by the (First) Synod of Ephesus and exiled to the Inner Oasis.[147]

5 Having fallen into this evil way of thinking, Marcian commanded a host of bishops to attend a synod. It was a long time since Nestorius had been sent into exile.[148] But he was still alive, so Marcian invited him, too.

6 On receiving the emperor's letter, Nestorius was struck by the angel of the Lord. His tongue was paralyzed and became infested with maggots, his face was devastated, and he died.[149]

145. 2 Kgs 22f.

146. Cf. Acts 8:9–24; CTh 16.5.66; John Rufus, *Proofs* 20, 42 [142]$3_{f.}$; *V. Petri Iberi* 76.

147. The Great Oasis, also called ἡ ἄνω Ὄασις, is in Libya, ca. 300 km west of Akhmim. The MSS have "Asia" for "Oasis," but see Socrates, *Eccl. hist.* 7.34.

148. In 435.

149. Zachariah Rhetor (*Eccl. hist.* 3.1, 1483–13) adds that this was a punishment for blasphemy against Mary, the mother of Jesus. See also John Rufus, *Proofs* 36, 84f. [484f.] (referring to Timothy of Alexandria's lost *Ecclesiastical History*); *V. Nestorii* 24f.; Eutychius 1033 B; Severus, *Synods* 5151–3 [51] ; Michael, *Chron.* 8.10.

§ 115 *The bishops accuse him falsely.*

1 The emperor wanted to summon Barsauma to the synod; but those bishops who followed the apostate Nestorius prostrated themselves before Marcian and the empress and urged them not to invite him. They feared him greatly, knowing that if he came, their apostasy would not be accepted.

2 In their cunning those deceitful bishops addressed the emperor and his consort as follows: "This Barsauma, who has the reputation of a righteous man, is in fact a leader of wizards and Magians. His 'great signs and miracles' are feats of sorcery; and it is by enchantments that he casts out evil spirits. His immoderate doctrine is a pack of Magian lies. If he comes to your synod, his magic spells will defeat both us and you."

3 When the emperor and his consort heard this, they conceived a great fear of Barsauma and abandoned their intention of inviting him. Instead, they looked askance at him and hated him with all their hearts.[150]

§ 116 *The synod of Chalcedon.*

1 The synod was held at Chalcedon in Bithynia. As soon as the bishops went into session, they leaned toward the very heresy which they had rejected in the reign of Theodosius. They could see that Marcian and his consort leaned toward this evil way of thinking and, to ingratiate themselves with them, made a volte-face, accepting the false doctrine of the two natures.

2 "Nature" (Syriac: *kyōnō*) is a name for something created. No Person of the Divinity is called a "nature," because He is considered to be of the Absolute Essence (Syriac: *ītūtō*, abstract noun derived from *īt*, "to exist"). Every creature is called a "nature," because it has been created (Syriac: *ettkīn*, passive of *akkīn*, cognate with the noun *kyōnō*); whereas one who is God is called an Absolute Being (Syriac: *ītyō*), because He exists absolutely (Syriac: *ītaw*, verb cognate with the nouns *ītūtō* and *ītyō*). It is not written that Christ was created, but that everything was created (Syriac: *mkōn*, passive participle of *akkīn*) by Him.[151]

150. Michael, *Chron.* 8.10.9f.

151. Cf. Jn 1:3.

This Christ therefore, who created (Syriac: *akkīn*) everything, cannot be called a "nature," because it is written concerning Him that whoever accepts his testimony confirms that He is truly God.[152]

3 So again he (John the Evangelist), in speaking about the same Christ, our Redeemer, said that the Father has confirmed that the Son of Man is truly God. So again, it has been said that "Christ is the God of all, to whom be praises and blessings forever and ever, Amen!"[153]

4 However, all of those bishops knew that the doctrine of the two natures is anathema; for it is written that "we have seen the glory of Christ, as of the Only One (Syriac: *īḥīdoyo*) who (comes) from the Father."[154] Those who use the appellation of the two natures cannot call Christ "single," because they say that there are two natures (in Him), perfect God and perfect human being.

5 No one whose tongue confesses this has any part or inheritance in the Only Son. The one Only Son cannot be called "two natures." When God bore witness from heaven concerning his Son while He was being baptized in the Jordan, He did not say: "These are my Sons and my Beloved Ones," as (one) who (speaks of) two. God, speaking from heaven, implied that He was one.[155]

6 Now not all of those bishops who were assembled in the city of Chalcedon actually strayed from the Faith, but (only) a few of them. All the rest held fast to the truth privately in their minds, but because they were afraid of the emperor, they wanted to ingratiate themselves with him. They feared human authority more than that of God.

7 Their case is comparable with what is written in the Gospel: "Many of the leaders of the Jews believed in Jesus, but were afraid, because of their fellow leaders, to confess Him openly."[156] For they (too) loved praise from human beings more than praise from God.[157]

8 The following prophetic utterance was fulfilled by those hypocritical bishops:

152. Jn 3:33.

153. Cf. 1 Pt 4:11, which actually reads (translating from the Syriac): "that God might be glorified in everything that you do through Jesus Christ, to whom belong praise and honor forever and ever, Amen."

154. Jn 1:14.

155. Mt 3:17; Mk 1:11; Lk 3:22.

156. Jn 3:1–21; 7:12f.

157. Cf. Jn 3:19.

God has stood up in the assembly of the angels;
From among the angels will He give judgment.
For how long will you give evil judgment
and respect the persons of wicked men?[158]
For I said: You are gods
and all of you are sons of the Most High.
Nevertheless you shall die like human beings;
and fall like one of the princes.[159]

9 Another inspired Scripture was also fulfilled by those priests who turned aside from the Truth: "They have all turned aside with one accord"[160] and earned contempt.

God will scatter the bones of those who ingratiate themselves with human beings. They have been put to shame—[161]

—because God has despised them.

§ 117 *Dioscorus, the bishop of Alexandria.*

1 Now Dioscorus, the bishop of Alexandria the Great, was not afraid of the emperor's authority and did not accept the contemptible doctrine of the apostates. Then he walked out of that wicked synod; and some other bishops walked out after him. The empress went out with many people in the night; and she came and prostrated herself at the feet of Dioscorus to make him agree to her will and to that of her husband.

2 The empress said to Dioscorus: "Accept the petition of your servant and do your daughter's will! For I am your servant and your daughter and all that I possess is yours." But Barsauma said to her: "Call me neither master, nor father! I am not your father any more than you are my daughter! What you possess is not mine! You have no fellowship with me, because you have left the Way of Truth and have followed the false teaching. That way lies darkness!"

3 The empress Pulcheria tried with many other words to persuade Dioscorus, but he was adamant. In the end she resorted to a

158. Ps 82:1f.
159. Ps 82:6f.
160. Cf. Ps 53:3.
161. Cf. Ps 53:5.

threat: "If you will not be persuaded, we shall take away your throne!" Dioscorus replied: "You may take away that wooden throne, but you cannot take away the throne which Christ has established for me in heaven."[162]

4 When the empress heard this, she went back home with a deep grievance. Shortly afterward, Dioscorus was sent into exile. He remained there for the rest of his life and died in exile. He departed from the world at a good age and was buried with honor.[163]

§ 118 Mari, the bishop of Qāra (?)[164] *in Arabia.*

1 Now Bishop Mari, (of Qāra?) in Arabia, had also suffered at this time. Putting on the seal of the Faith, this holy man stood up among the bishops while they were in session and asked: "What has this assembly of devils done?"

2 The apostates were greatly troubled and ground their teeth at him. They threw a cloak around the holy man's neck and, dragging him into the middle, began kicking him in the stomach, until he spat blood and began to vomit excrement. They went on abusing him like this until he seemed to have no life left in him, then threw him into the street for dead.

3 After a while, however, he recovered, went back in, and, standing in the middle of the assembly, cried out again: "What has this assembly of devils done?"

4 Again they threw a cloak around his neck to drag him with and beat him up even worse than the first time. Now Mari was an old man, but by dint of fasting and prayer he had stayed strong, for he had forsworn, among other foods, bread, wine, and oil. Nevertheless, those bishops dragged him around and tormented him, then threw him into prison.

5 When night came, they took him out of jail and left him outside the city. Mari later went to Rome, where he departed from the world and was buried by the Christians.

162. Cf. Lk 22:28–30.

163. This chapter is closely related to *V. Dioscori* 10, 5511–568.

164. The second consonant may have been *D* or *Z*, not *R*: all three variants are attested.

§ 119 *Marcian sends out a great army because of the division (occasioned by Chalcedon).*

1 At this time of unrest, a Roman army, sent by the emperor, slaughtered at least thirty thousand in Alexandria. All of these died as Confessors.

2 Marcian sent another army to Jerusalem. Those who were slaughtered in the region of Palestine in those days were about three thousand five hundred, most of whom were priests. They, too, died for Christ.

3 Others were exiled, imprisoned, deprived of their income, driven from their monasteries, expelled from their regions, or made strangers to their kin-groups; yet others fled to the wilderness, or were forced to take refuge in another country. All these, too, were Confessors of Christ's Cross.

4 As for Barsauma, by word and by deed he was making a greater effort than anyone else, teaching people everywhere not to obey the emperor's command, nor to accept the apostates' words, nor to turn aside from the true Faith, nor to call the Only (Syriac: *iḥīdoyo*) Son[165] "two natures," nor to posit a division in the One true Son; nor to deny the crucifixion of the Lord Christ, who is true God from true God, the Son of the Essence (Syriac: *ītūto*) of his Father, to whom be praise and honor forever and ever, Amen!

§ 120 *The bishops slander him.*

1 Now those bishops who had fallen away from the true Faith were afraid that Barsauma would turn people everywhere against the false doctrine of the two natures. They said to one another: "What can we do? To sin is human. We strayed from the true Way out of fear of the emperor's authority. What we have written, whether well or badly, we have written.[166]

2 "What we have done, whether sinfully or justly, we have done. If we admit to the people that we were wrong to sign, the imperial couple will persecute us. If we are silent and discreet, the monk Barsauma will expose us. If we allow him to live, our crime will not remain a secret for long. He is going to go around telling everyone what we

165. Jn 1:14.
166. Cf. Jn 19:22.

have put our names to. He is going to write letters exposing our deed to men in distant countries, too. The people obey him. Us they pelt with stones!

3 "What is more, he is on his way to Greater Rome, where he is going to tell the emperor Valentinian, who is going to listen to him and send a force to burn us alive. This emperor, Marcian, is feeble; he will not be able to save us from death. Come, then! Let us think of a way to kill Barsauma, before he kills us all!"[167]

4 For these reasons the bishops were suspicious of Barsauma and began to hate him. Every day, in the presence of the emperor Marcian and his consort, they slandered him; and they spoke against him in the presence of high officials, bringing accusations against him, framing him with malicious indictments, imputing great sins to him.

5 They told lies against him and blamed him for their own crimes. They smeared him with their own repulsiveness. Whatever they themselves were in the habit of doing, they began to say that Barsauma did the same.

6 They even attributed to him the hateful doctrine which they had embraced. They sent liars to preach in churches and in front of the crowds, speaking against him in the people's hearing. They brought deceitful witnesses into the assemblies and the streets to give false witness against him everywhere.

7 Where they saw that the doctrine of the two natures was accepted, they, too, confessed two and called Barsauma an apostate, "because (they said) he refuses to accept the doctrine of the two natures." But again, where they saw that the two natures were not accepted, they slandered him, saying that it was he that taught the two.

8 Where they saw that people denied the crucifixion of the Son, they said: "Barsauma has departed from the truth. He blasphemously claims that the Son of God was crucified." Then again, where they saw that people confessed that it was the Son of God who died, they accused him falsely, saying: "Barsauma teaches that the man who was crucified was not the Son of God."

9 Where they saw that people received Nestorius, they used to say, to appease them: "This apostate Barsauma refuses to accept the holy Nestorius." Then again, where there were people who anathematized

167. Cf. Michael, *Chron.* 8.14; Gregory, *Chron. eccl.* 1.179–82.

Nestorius, they used slanderously to say: "This liar Barsauma teaches the doctrine of Nestorius."

10 They did this to make everyone hate Barsauma, accusing him besides of many crimes, so as to scandalize the people. I cannot write down in this book the many accusations which they made against him. There are too many to be counted; and some of them are too offensive to be read out in the people's hearing.

11 But mark my words! Because they have gone so far as to accuse him, they themselves are going to be put on trial. Their testimony is going to be exposed as false in front of Christ's throne.

§ 121 *The emperor Marcian orders his arrest.*

1 Now the emperor Marcian and his wife were troubled and angry in the extreme. Marcian sent an order, full of menace, to a certain count (κόμης) who had been created for the Entrance to the Sea, telling him to arrest Barsauma and bring him to the City.

2 The slanderers had been telling the imperial couple: "If you leave Barsauma alive, he will go up to Rome and get the emperor Valentinian to send and cut off your heads and throw us into the sea. If the leading men of the City make a stand to support you, Valentinian will start an all-out war and burn your city down."

3 It was because of their fear of the Romans that Marcian and his wife tried to get Barsauma into their palace. In their stupidity they thought that if only he would come to them, fear would make him weak and he would acquiesce in their way of thinking.

§ 122 *The seventy-third sign. A demon is expelled from a Roman soldier.*

1 When the command of the emperor reached to the count of the Straits (Syriac: *esṭīno;* cf. Greek: τῶν στενῶν), he took a large number of soldiers and went out to arrest Barsauma. He caught up with him near a city called Tenedos.[168]

168. We later come across a count of the Black Sea Straits at Abydos, on the Hellespont (Fiona K. Haarer, *Anastasius I: Politics and Empire in the Late Roman World*, ARCA, Classical and Medieval Texts, Papers and Monographs 46 [Cambridge: F. Cairns, 2006], 218–19); it may be that Barsauma was arrested near the main town on the island of Tenedos. This would explain why he was thought to be on his way to Rome (§ 121.2).

2 Now the soldiers whom the emperor had commanded to arrest Barsauma did not know him by sight. One of them, a strongly built man who tended to violence, had long been possessed by a demon. All of a sudden this man's hands and feet were locked together. He stood there, like one crucified or turned into a wooden post, and was on the point of being suffocated by that demon.

3 Barsauma came up and blew on him; immediately the devil left him to make its escape from Barsauma. Then that soldier fell down and performed an act of worship in front of God's Slave.[169] He was healed and experienced no more harm.

4 When the soldiers saw what had happened, they fell down on their faces in front of Christ's champion (ἀθλητής). Many other signs also were performed in those days by his agency. Then they brought him to the Imperial City.

§ 123 The seventy-fourth sign. A magistrate, cursed by him, dies.

1 The emperor Marcian commanded his magistrate to have Barsauma brought in to his presence with haste and not to let any of his disciples enter with him, so that he might be disoriented and frightened by the numerous people there.

2 So Barsauma entered the law court on his own; the attendants seized him and stood him in front of the magistrate.

3 Then the magistrate began to speak harshly and menacingly. "You are Barsauma," he said, "the wizard and false guide; the emperor's enemy; the murderer of bishops."

4 Barsauma said: "I am Barsauma, the Christian. I have not abandoned the Word of truth, nor denied Christ, as you have. I am no enemy of believing emperors, no murderer of true priests. I am, however, the enemy of rebellious emperors, a hater of unbelieving priests. I have never killed a bishop. The Lord, however, will kill a priest who denies the truth."

5 When the magistrate heard this, he was was deeply disturbed and very angry. He shouted out loud: "By my office, by the emperor's life, by the honor of his throne, I swear that I will throw you into a place where there is no water."

169. Cf. Heb 3:5.

6 At this, Barsauma laughed. He wagged his head and, using freedom of speech, cried: "Hah! You have forsworn yourself and the emperor's authority! Your oath cannot be kept! You can throw me into a place where there is no water. But God, the Lord of sources, will be there. When He sees that water is needed for my use, either He will cause it to rain, or He will make water well up out of the earth for me.

7 "Throw me, if you can, into a place where there is no God! Then, perhaps, you will be able to keep your oath."

8 The magistrate retorted: "I can do just that! I can cast you into a place where there is no God." "There is no place that is empty of God," said Barsauma, "except for the chair on which you sit and the throne of your wicked emperor! And if you throw me into one of those two places, God will come to that place also for my sake."

9 This made the magistrate even angrier. He threatened Barsauma: "I shall cut you up into small pieces and throw your flesh out, limb by limb."

10 At this, Barsauma clasped his hands together behind him, turned his head to one side, and showed the judge his throat, shouting: "O basest of judges and most shameful of men, for all your threats and those of your emperor, who is just as base and shameful, do not you have even the smallest blade with which to cut this soft throat of mine and rid yourself of me?"

11 The magistrate was astonished. He groaned inwardly, too much afraid to answer.

12 Warming to his theme, Barsauma continued: "Evil and rebellious slave! In your arrogance you make threats and lord it over me. Your master, the emperor Marcian, did not dare to remain seated in my presence. As for you, not only do you remain seated in my presence, you even presume to judge me! As Christ, whom I serve, is true to me, you shall not judge any other case in this world! The case of God's Slave,[170] Barsauma, will be your last!"

13 This pronouncement struck terror into the magistrate's heart. He shook at the joints. He stood up from the bench on which he was sitting and ran to the emperor Marcian, trembling all over.

170. Cf. Heb 3:5.

14 He undid his belt and laid it down in front of the emperor. "Here in your presence," he said, "I lay down all the honors which you have given me. I am going to die. Barsauma has killed me." "What has he done to you?" asked the emperor.

15 "He put a curse on me," the magistrate replied, "and killed me. The curse is like a sharp arrow, which has struck my heart and broken it. I have this sharp, stabbing pain in my heart. I can feel my soul fluttering to make her escape from my body."

16 The magistrate sent the following instructions to his wife: "Go quickly to Barsauma and plead with him on my behalf! I am dying!"

17 His wife hurried out to find Barsauma; her slaves went in ahead of her and told him: "My lord, your servant and daughter is outside. She has come to worship you."

18 Hearing this, he gave them the following message for her: "Do not put yourself to the trouble of coming to see me, because I shall not receive you! You would do better to prepare a funeral for your husband!"

19 But she insisted and sent word to him again: "I know that, if Your Grace so desires, my husband will not die. If he is healed and retains his post, he will do your bidding."

20 Here is Barsauma's reply: "You had better believe what I say: your husband will never judge another case. Very soon his soul will be taken, because he has ingratiated himself with wickedness by persecuting Christ, who is going swiftly to take him out of the world to stop him oppressing his servants."

21 That very day the magistrate became ill and was confined to his bed; he died a few days later.

§ 124 The emperor Marcian sends a prefect to him.

1 Then the emperor was very much afraid. He summoned the highest prefect (Syriac: [*h*]*ūparko rabbo;* cf. Greek: μέγιστος ὕπαρχος) and said: "Come, go to the archimandrite (Syriac: *rīš dayro*) Barsauma and say to him in my name: 'The emperor urges you to take what you want from the treasury, both for your own honor and for the provision of your monastery, and return in peace and honor to your monastery! No one will do you any harm. Only do not put a curse on me!'"

2 Now that prefect feared the Lord; moreover, he loved and honored the Christians. He came to see Barsauma in the place where he was imprisoned and went into his room in faith, bending his head before him and asking for his peace. He did not presume to sit down in his presence, but remained standing, listening to his teaching.

3 After listening to him for a long time, he said: "My lord, the imperial couple implore Your Grace not to put a curse on them. Instead, they beg Your Holiness to accept from them gifts for your monastery and rations of corn for your brethren. You may return in honor and peace to your monastery!"

4 At this, Barsauma asked: "Did not the emperor Theodosius urge me to accept gifts from him, altar-vessels at the least, and I refused?" The prefect answered: "I know you did."

5 Then Barsauma said: "If the emperor Theodosius, who was true in his faith and whom I loved, urged me to accept altar-vessels and I refused, how should I accept secular gifts from this Marcian, my enemy, who denies the truth and whom I hate?"

6 When the prefect heard this, he inclined his head before the champion (ἀθλητής) and received his blessing. Then he went to the emperor and told him everything. The emperor insisted: "Go and urge the archimandrite Barsauma to leave the City. If he stays here for many days, he will turn the people against me. I am afraid there is going to be sedition (Syriac: *esṭasīn* = στάσις) against me in the City."

7 The prefect replied: "You sent me the first time with the brief to use persuasion. I cannot now go with the brief to use compulsion. I am afraid he will be angry with me and curse me. Use another messenger! If I go to see him, it will be to receive his blessing, that he might pray for me."

§ 125 Marcian sends a Patricius, meaning "a father of emperors," to him.

1 Then the emperor Marcian spoke with one of his great men, whose title was "Father of emperors." This man had earlier been a friend of Barsauma's. The emperor said to him: "Come, go to your friend, Barsauma, and tell him not to curse me! Advise him to leave the City and return with honor to his monastery!"

2 So the man spoke with Barsauma and begged him to accept many gifts; but he refused everything. So he simply implored him to depart from the City.

§ 126 The seventy-fifth sign. Fire breaks out in the City.

1 Barsauma accepted his petition. But he was not yet quite gone when fire broke out in the City. It quickly turned into a great conflagration and destroyed many houses and great palaces.

2 Now there was a certain believing woman there, who sent the following message to Barsauma: "My lord, have mercy on me! Pray for me and my house and all that I have! The flames have come right up to my house and there is no one who can help me."

3 Barsauma put some water into a cauldron, blessed it, made the sign of the cross over it in Christ's name and sent it to that woman with this message: "Take this water in faith and sprinkle it on the door and walls of your house!" She carried out these instructions.

4 The fire now surrounded her house, and the blaze was lapping against its walls. Yet the flames did not take hold of the house; not even a straw of it was destroyed. The fire burned down all of the houses which surrounded it. Great buildings swayed and fell to the ground. But that house in the middle remained standing, unshaken.

5 The woman came and fell at his feet, thanking him in the sight of all.

§ 127 He leaves the Imperial City.

1 Then Barsauma departed from the Imperial City and came to Nicomedia, where he stayed throughout that winter, under military guard. He persuaded a great number of people there not to depart from the true Faith, as preached by the blessed apostles and confirmed by the three hundred and eighteen bishops who were assembled in the city of Nicaea in the days of the true and righteous emperor Constantine, who deserves a good commemoration.

2 God's true Slave[171] preached this same Faith and divine doctrine wherever he went; accordingly, he taught it at Nicomedia. He also performed other signs there, but I have not written them down in this book.

171. Cf. Heb 3:5.

§ 128 *The seventy-sixth sign. The empress Pulcheria, cursed by him, dies.*

1 The following summer, the emperor Marcian sent a command to Barsauma to return in peace to his monastery. The empress also wrote him a letter: "We begged and urged you to be our father and instructor, but you refused. So we command you now to return in peace to your monastery. We shall not come to you, nor you to us. We will have nothing to do with you, because you hate us."

2 Barsauma sent back the following message: "I am the slave of the Crucified. It is Christ's will that I go in peace to my native country. It is not at your command that I go to my monastery, nor am I dismissed from this place at the bidding of your husband. It is the will of the Living God and of his Son.

3 "As the Crucified, whom you have doubted and denied, is true to me, you will vacate your throne. Only then, in all serenity, shall I enter my monastery."

4 Then Barsauma left Nicomedia for Syria. He was about a day's journey from his monastery when a messenger, who had followed him on swift horses,[172] caught up with him and, leaping to the ground, prostrated himself in front of him.

5 "My lord," he said, "God has fulfilled your prediction! The empress who hated you fell into a cruel torment, which ended with her swallowing her own tongue and dying in agony." At this, Barsauma lifted his eyes to heaven, praising Christ and weeping great tears.

§ 129 *The seventy-seventh sign. A man is bitten by a mad dog and healed by the sign of the cross.*

1 Only then did he reach his monastery, where a great number of people had come out to welcome him back. He was teaching these when, from a certain village, they brought him a man who had been bitten by a mad dog and was now possessed by many demons. These left the man the moment Barsauma rebuked them, and he went home, whole and rejoicing.

172. Cf. Hb 1:8.

§ 130 *Many signs.*

1 The possessed arrived from all directions, and their demons were exorcised. Signs of various kinds occurred. Many sick people were healed by his prayers.

§ 131 *The seventy-eighth sign. He sends his disciple to stop a fatal contagion.*

1 A few days later, in a certain famous town, a contagious disease appeared. Some people from that town went to see him and tried to persuade him to go and pray there and prevent the disease from spreading. But he summoned instead the disciple who had seen those astonishing apparitions and addressed him as follows.

2 "My son, it is written in the Law of Moses that, when a plague suddenly broke out in the wilderness in the camp of the Sons of Israel, the Lord told Moses to say to his brother, Aaron: 'Fill your censer with burning coals and incense and run through the camp toward the plague!' Holding the censer in his hand, Aaron stood between the dead and the living, and the angel of death, seeing him, turned away from the people.[173]

3 "So take the oil of prayer in your hand and go at a run to the town where this contagious disease has broken out. Enter the church and pray there, burning incense and offering the oblations. Then our Lord will make the disease turn away from that community likewise!" That disciple did as Barsauma told him; and from that moment the spread of the disease was halted.

§ 132 *The seventy-ninth sign. A plague is halted by his prayers.*

1 A few days later they came to Barsauma from another settlement, saying: "My lord, have pity on us and come and pray in our village! A virulent plague has broken out in it!" This time, Barsauma granted their request and went back with them.

2 They were about to enter the area of the threshing-floors when some men from that settlement appeared, bearing a man on a bier. He was still just breathing. They set him down in front of him and,

173. Nm 16:46–48.

grasping him by the hand, he raised him up in Christ's name before their very eyes.

3 Now a priest from another place happened to be present. This man, influenced by the bishops who hated Barsauma, had his doubts about him. But when he saw him raising up a man who had been given up for dead, he was amazed and afraid.

4 Out loud, he said: "Now I know that you have not strayed from the Faith. I acknowledge that everything the bishops say about you is a downright lie. Everyone who maligns you and blasphemes against your true doctrine will meet with his fate. Even his memory will be damned." That priest hurried about, witnessing to everyone who crossed his path. As for Barsauma, he prayed in that village, and the plague was halted.

§ 133 The bishops send a deceitful letter.

1 The bishops wrote a letter of excommunication and sent it to that district so that no one would associate with him. All the inhabitants of the district were assembled in one place when the letter arrived and was read out in their hearing. It contained terrible menaces and laid many curses on anyone who refused. It threatened such a person with punishment by the emperor himself and made scandalous accusations against Barsauma.

2 Then one of the leading men of that country said: "My brothers, you all know that I have an only son who fell ill and was close to death. We had given him up for dead. With the help of others, I bore him to Barsauma's monastery. I wanted to bury him there. Not for a moment did I imagine he could come back to life.

3 "But when Barsauma prayed over him, my dead son came back to life and fully recovered his health. Here he is, standing in front of you. Let the bishops who despise Barsauma come here and pray over one dead goat-kid! If they can bring even that back to life, I will reject Barsauma and accept them! My family and I, at least, will not be separated from Christ's Slave.'

4 This speech was followed by an almighty clamor.

"We will not deny God's Slave!"[174] the people shouted.

"We will not desert the Christ of our country!

174. Cf. Heb 3:5.

"We will not doubt the one who repairs the spiritual defenses of our region!

"We are not to be separated from the one who keeps harm from our land!

"We will not be cut off from the physician of our diseases!

"We will not be prevented from associating with the healer of our sick!"

§ 134 *The eightieth sign. A deacon with rigid fingers.*

1 This was the answer to the bishops' letter. When they received it, they were at a loss what to do about Barsauma. Then they sent an order that all those in the villages and the monasteries who were in holy orders should assemble in one place and anathematize him.

2 A certain deacon, who was also an archimandrite, took up his stance in the middle of the assembly and shouted out: "Fathers, listen!"—and he stretched out his right hand so that everyone could see it.

3 "Many of you know the facts. These fingers were once rigid. I could not bring them together. But then I showed them to Barsauma. He made the sign of the cross over them in Christ's name (lit. "sealed them in the name of the Crucified"). Then he covered them with spittle from his mouth. Immediately, I found they were no longer rigid. I could move them. They were healed! This happened in the sight of some here present today.

4 "This I tell you: So long as I have this healthy hand before my eyes, I refuse to say 'Anathema to the man who healed it!' Anyone who denies him will be denied in turn! Anyone who says 'Anathema!' is anathema himself!"

5 Every man who heard this was ashamed, and not one presumed to answer him back. Then they refrained from the thing they had intended.

§ 135 *The eighty-first sign. A paralyzed woman regains her health.*

1 The following day, many people were standing there, disputing with him, when some men from a distant country appeared, carrying a woman of about thirty years, whose hands and feet had been paralyzed and rigid since childhood. Barsauma made the sign of the cross

over her hands and her legs, and she was healed. Those disputing with him hung their heads in shame and slunk away.

§ 136 *The eighty-second sign. A devil speaks through a woman against those who deny the truth.*

1 Another day, when others were standing there, disputing with him, a woman from a distant country, who was possessed by a devil, appeared, haranguing loudly long before she reached him.

2 "These days," it was her voice, but it was the devil who was speaking, "the bishops are our friends. Now it is you, Barsauma, burned and desiccated as you are, who are our greatest enemy, the persecutor of our race. The great zeal of your fiery nature bound me with a band of fire. It has brought me from a distant country to be punished in your presence. Were it not for your prayers, we would now be in control everywhere.

3 "Those bishops who have become our brothers and intimates opened the door for us to enter into the world. But you, impudent man, covered with bruises from the stones that have been thrown at you, refuse to keep quiet and even persist in trying to lock that door, the door of apostasy, which the bishops, our friends, have opened for us."

4 When those disputing with him heard the unclean devil's speech, they prostrated themselves in front of Barsauma, each sobbing on his own account.

§ 137 *The eighty-third sign. A consecrated woman,*[175] *possessed by an impure devil.*

1 Another day, many people were assembled around him, many of whom were arguing that the Body of Christ was like a human body.

2 All of a sudden, an impure demon shouted out, using the voice of a certain woman: "I am Satan, the spiritual Master of the Left Hand. I am he that tempted Christ, the Son of God, in the wilderness. I am he that dared to say to Him: 'Fall down and worship me!'[176] His compulsion has bound me and brought me from the abysses of the Earth, that I might be judicially tortured by the burning seal of Barsauma,

175. Syriac: *ba(r)th qyomo*, "a daughter of the covenant."

176. Cf. Mt 4:9; Lk 4:7.

the victim of persecution. It is under compulsion that I declare the truth, although I hate it.

3 "If the body of Jesus is like a human body, which human being has broken his body and given it as food to his friends? And if the blood of the Crucified, the Firstborn, is like the blood of the human race, what human blood can atone for sin?"[177] The devil said this.

4 Then he added the following: "I am no herald of the truth, but its enemy. It is the compulsion of the Crucified which is forcing me to tell the truth." When those who had been disputing with him heard this they were even more ashamed.

§ 138 *The eighty-fourth sign. A man possessed by an evil spirit is healed.*

1 Another day, when many were arguing with him, some Cappadocians appeared, bringing a man possessed by an evil spirit, who was covered with suppurating sores from his toenails to his scalp. He was an appalling sight.

2 Barsauma made the sign of the cross over him with spittle from his mouth. The pus ceased to flow, and the sores dried up and became like fish-scales, with raw flesh visible underneath. These scales gradually worked loose and fell to the ground, and the man's skin was healed.

3 Those who had been disputing with Barsauma were put to shame in the eyes of all bystanders; if they continued to disagree with him, it was only out of envy.

§ 139 *The eighty-fifth sign. The hand and tongue of a preacher who maligns him are disabled.*

1 Now there was a priest in another district who was a preacher with a large following. He preached in the churches and the monasteries and taught many the text of the Scriptures. He had been a friend of Barsauma's, but he had suddenly changed his mind and now disapproved of him.

2 All at once he fell ill and took to his bed. His friends said: "You ought not to disapprove of God's Slave.[178] We know he holds to the truth and you yourself bear witness that he has not departed from the

177. Cf. Barhebraeus, *Candelabra* 4.6.2–3 (ed. 234f., 242f.).

178. Cf. Heb 3:5.

true Faith. Everyone acknowledges that it is the bishops who are in the wrong."

3 The moment he stretched out his hand to speak blasphemy and opened his mouth to malign Barsauma, his hand withered, the flesh of his arm fell away, and his tongue split and dropped out. Soon afterward he died in agony. Many were afraid, but the apostates were confused by their error.[179]

§ 140 The eighty-sixth sign. A priest who blasphemes against him dies.

1 Satan's spirit entered a village-priest, filling him with error, so that he blasphemed. He put a wooden bar in the door of a monastery and shouted: "I am going to destroy this monastery, because the wicked Barsauma has prayed here and made it unclean."

2 This priest was still maligning Barsauma when the angel of the Lord suddenly struck him and threw him over. A burning fire fell on him and began to torment him. "I beg of you, Barsauma," he screamed, "have mercy on me and give me relief from this torment!"

3 Then, still screaming, he addressed his fellow villagers: "I beg of you all on my knees, show mercy toward me in my predicament! Let one of you go quickly to the oratory he made in such and such a place, take some of the earth on which he stood and bring it to me! I shall take refuge in Barsauma and be delivered from this hell in which I am burning."

4 But though the priest implored them, the people would not listen. They took pleasure in his distress and refused to send anyone to that place. Not long afterward he gave up the ghost.

§ 141 The eighty-seventh sign. Another priest maligns him and dies for it.

1 There was a priest-monk whom all the bishops loved—his maternal uncle was a well-known chorepiscopus—whom they authorized to incite the masses to persecute Barsauma.

2 One Sunday, when that priest was offering up the oblation in the church of a certain town, he took up his stance on the dais in front

179. There is wordplay in the original between *doḥlīn*, "afraid," and *dlīḥīn*, "confused."

of the altar, lifted up the pyx, and made this proclamation to the people: "Anathema to anyone who associates with the apostate Barsauma!"

3 The whole congregation answered with a single voice: "Anathema to you and to all your associates!" Then they walked out of the church-building, leaving him alone. After a little time he came out into the street and shouted at the elders: "May God do thus unto me and more, if I do not clap chains and collars around your necks and take you to Antioch!"

4 "As the Christ whom Barsauma preaches is true to us," replied those elders, "you will never see Antioch again!" Furious, the priest mounted his she-mule and left that town.

5 He had not gone far when the wrath of God suddenly struck him. His neck-muscles collapsed, and his joints shook. The people of the first village he came to had to help him to dismount, and immediately he fell to the ground in agony.

6 Now the priest of that village took pleasure in his distress, because he had been persecuted for his Faith. He and his congregation all gave thanks to God, because they were on Barsauma's side.

7 The priest who was in torment implored the other to send a message to Barsauma, begging him to forgive his offense and pray for his life. But that village-priest replied: "As the Lord lives, I will not send him any message, nor will I ask him to pray for you!"

8 The priest who was in agony now turned to the people: "I beg of you, have mercy on me! Let someone go to my lord Barsauma! I know that mercy dwells in him. He does not return evil for enmity. Send someone to him. The moment he prays for me, I shall recover, I know it! Then I shall repay you for your respect. I will give the man who goes to him whatever he wants."

9 But the priest of that village said to his people: "Anathema to anyone who goes and pleads with Barsauma on behalf of this man! Leave the blasphemer to die an evil death, the recompense of his blasphemy!" After suffering great torments, that priest gave up the ghost.

§ 142 Many signs.

1 Too many signs were performed at this time for them all to be written down here. We have written down those which are edifying with respect to the true Faith.

§ 143 *The deceitful letters which the apostates sent to him.*

1 Seeing that all their efforts had ended in shameful failure, the apostates now plotted to have Barsauma assassinated. They instructed one of their friends, a bishop, to kill him in an ambush. Having mustered about two thousand men on the mountain, this man concealed them beside a powerful river which flowed between cliffs too steep to climb.

2 Then, as a blind, they wrote the following letter, insincerely offering peace to Barsauma: "To the teacher of the truth and preacher of the Faith, the shepherd of human beings and father of us all and master of the mourners, Barsauma, most peaceful greetings!

3 "Sir, we thank the chosen status of your victorious person that the sin that we committed in error has been revealed to us. We acknowledge all the evil we have done. Now we understand and know in truth that you teach the way of justice, no error. But we are afraid to come to Your Holiness, in case the inhabitants of the country come out and stone us.

4 "So, my lord, we beg of Your Holiness that Your Grace might take the trouble to come to us, so that we may confess our sins in your presence and give our assent to the truth of your Faith."

5 When Barsauma received this letter, he was delighted, for the deceit of those damned men had not yet been revealed to him.

§ 144 *A disciple of his has a vision.*

1 One of his disciples, though, had received a revelation concerning their deceit one night. The Lord showed that disciple everything that the apostates were planning to do. He told two of his friends about the trap which the enemy had prepared, but he concealed it from his master.

2 When Barsauma went to meet those liars, the bishop and his confidants had hidden sticks behind the altar, intending to take him into the church alone and kill him there.

3 "If we can trick him into entering the church," they told each other, "we can beat him with the sticks. If he is unwilling to enter the church alone, the men we have concealed can come and kill him openly." This had also been shown to that disciple in every detail.

4 Those deceivers sent another long petition to Barsauma. At the same time certain respectable persons, instructed by them, gave him a message: "My lord, leave your brethren where they are and come to us on your own, secretly! Let just one disciple come with you! To begin with, we want to hold secret conference with you inside the church. Afterward we shall confess openly to our offense in front of the people."

5 Barsauma himself was willing to do this; but the disciple who knew the secret intentions of the deceivers said to him in front of those men: "Master, every day, as our father, you give the orders. Today, I give them. Stay here in the open with the brethren! I shall go to them secretly!"

6 He said this because he knew it was him and his master they wanted to kill. But they began to make dire threats against him, because he opposed them more than all the rest. The people who had been sent refused to take him, so they went back and Barsauma stayed with the brethren.

7 Then they sent others more important than the first, bringing a long petition. The disciple who knew their secrets answered them as before. They sent as many as ten times; and each time the disciple who had learned their intentions dismissed them with the same words as the first time. They were furious with him, but they did not know what to say.

8 In the end, in great anger, they said: "It is you that will not allow your master to make peace in the land! You are to blame for the discord between the parties today." "Your love is enmity to God," that disciple retorted. "Your insincere peace will rebound on you like a conflagration of wrath."

9 The reason why the disciple did not reveal the apostates' secrets to Barsauma is that he knew his master would leap at the chance of dying, if he knew that they wanted to kill him.

10 For some time that disciple had known how glad he would have been to die for the truth's sake. Barsauma had already hungered and thirsted for this in his youth; now, as an old man, he still yearned for it. This was why he hid from him the knowledge which had been revealed to him.

§ 145 *The apostates stone him, but he does not die.*

1 In the end, the apostates' messengers came to Barsauma and said: "Dismiss the brethren who are with you! Let them go wherever

they will! As for you, whether you want to or not, you are going to die now." He thought they were joking; but they swore by all that is holy that he was going to be killed that same day: "Any minute now your blood is going to be shed."

2 At this, inwardly, he jumped for joy. His mind was delighted. His face lit up and seemed to flash like lightning. Yes, he was filled with gladness and praised Christ. He lifted up his eyes to heaven in thanksgiving and made the following speech to the brethren who were with him.

3 "My sons, you know that it was for an opportunity like this that I went down to Persia long ago. But there among the pagans no one would kill me.[180] It was for this that I traveled in distant countries, but nowhere did I meet with this opportunity.

4 "But now that, God willing, I have found what I have been looking for, I ought indeed to give thanks to our Lord, who has fulfilled the desire of my heart. What I went in quest of with so much trouble, He has given me with no effort today.

5 "So now, whoever wishes to follow me, let him follow with joy; and whoever wishes to go, let him go in peace! Only, my sons, see that you take up no sticks and throw no stones! Curse no one! Do not indulge in insults! Do not resist the murderers! Do not argue! Do just what you see me do!"

6 Having said this, he ran toward the murderers with a spring in his step. His shining face was like that of one jostling to enter at the gate of the Kingdom.

7 His persecutors hurriedly selected a place in which to stone him. They all came and stood on the bank of a stream, where there were many pebbles. They had brought with them the men who had been lying in wait in the ravine and many others. These stood on one side of the stream, while he approached from the other side.

8 Many women and children were watching from a distance with tears in their eyes, shouting: "You, who won a great victory on the cross, help your worshipper, Barsauma!"

9 Barsauma had reached the edge of the water and was in a hurry to cross over quickly, so that those people could stone him; for he thought his last hour had come.

180. Cf. § 110.9.

10 But that disciple did not allow him to go in among them. He overtook him at a run and, stopping on the bank of the stream, made the following speech.

11 "Turn round, master! Look eastward and pray! Bless the sons who are following you, like a flock of lambs running into the hands of the slaughterer! Bless your other sons, who are far away from here! Do not deprive them of their reward for the trials they have borne with you! Remember that they have rejected their families and committed themselves to you!

12 "Bless this district, in which you grew up! Remember how the local people always bowed down to you! Give absolution to these people who are going to stone you! Pay off the debts of your friend, Stephen![181] Forgive everyone who has ever offended against you! Release from his bond everyone you have put under a ban!"

13 The disciple who said this was the same as had had the vision of his master being stoned. He realized now that all this had come to pass to fulfill his prayer "that his eyes might see the people stoning him."

14 As for Barsauma, turning round to look at the disciples who were following him, he said: "See to it, my sons, that you do as I told you! Let no curse or insult come out of your mouths! Take up neither stone nor stick against any man! Do exactly as you see me do!"

15 He was still saying this when the men who were going to stone him called to his disciples: "Leave your master to die! Flee! It is him we want to kill!" And they set about stoning him.

16 Now the stones which they threw at him were smooth river pebbles. One man threw a white stone which hit Barsauma above his left eye, giving off a loud report. Those who heard it thought that it had broken his skull. But all of a sudden something just like that stone came out of the air and struck the man who had thrown it and broke his skull, devastating his face and pushing his left eye out of its socket.[182]

17 His disciple was standing in front of him with his right arm around his neck. Now he embraced him and spoke to him: "By the life of the Crucified One, whom you love, let this much be enough for you!

181. Cf. Acts 6f.

182. Cf. Ex 21:24; Dt 32:35; Mt 5:38f.; Rom 12:19.

18 "It is not the men who are stoning you. They are feeble. It is our Lord, making your wish come true. Today He has fulfilled the request you made some time ago, that He allow you to see the people stoning you. Master, if you die at the hands of these sinners, this country will be devastated by your assassination. I know it! Fire will come down from heaven and consume it, as it consumed Sodom together with all its inhabitants."

19 But Barsauma said to his disciple: "Let them stone me, my son!" He was unwilling to let him go; but Barsauma clasped his hands behind him and bowed deeply in front of those who were stoning him, so his disciples did exactly the same, as did the other religious who had come to watch. Most of the stones, however, were thrown at him.

§ 146 *The eighty-eighth sign.*

1 The disciple who had his right hand around Barsauma's neck stretched out his other hand against the men who were stoning him. Many stones struck his hand, his face, his head, and his shoulders. All those stones fell down and piled up around them, until a great pile had accumulated there. Now that disciple did not feel the pain of a single one of those stones, nor was a single scratch to be seen on his body.[183]

§ 147 *The eighty-ninth sign.*

1 Suddenly, an east wind, or something like it, got up and bowled those stoning Barsauma right over. "Run!" they called to one another; and, terrified, they began to flee.

§ 148 *The ninetieth sign. A devil speaks through a woman and puts the apostates to shame.*

1 When the people had run away and put a distance between themselves and that place, he straightened up from his bowing position and moved upward to a vantage point, beautiful, splendid, and high. Others were making their way to the place in which he had been stoned.

2 Among these was a woman seated on a she-mule, who had an unclean devil in her. This woman dismounted, took some soil from that place, and threw it up in the air. Then she began to shout

183. Cf. § 93.

with her hands clasped behind her and walked backward up the mountainside.

3 The men who had been stoning Barsauma watched her from a distance, while she climbed up toward him and shouted at them: "You men who have stoned Barsauma, it is you I am talking to! This is the entrance by which you can go in before the Throne of Christ, whom you have denied!"

4 The people, hearing this, began to weep; and their groans went up to heaven. They began to climb toward him from all sides. There on the mountain he spoke to them of many things.[184]

5 His enemies held their position until evening. But at sunset dark clouds covered the sky, and it began to rain heavily.

6 God put fear into the hearts of those who had stoned him, and they began to say to one another: "Let us flee from Barsauma this very minute! If we stay here tonight, he will come over and kill us!" Then and there those apostates got up, too much afraid to have their supper.

7 The river rushed down wildly between steep slopes, surrounded by many rocky cliffs, with thorny bushes around it which were entangled with one another; and they fled along its course. It was so steep and wild that a man could not easily walk down it, even in the daytime.

8 All that night they were in difficulties. It was pitch-dark, and there was a torrential rainstorm. They thought Barsauma was pursuing them, and fled headlong in fear and trepidation, tripping up and falling on the rocks. All night long they were getting tied up in knots and encountering difficulties on the steep mountainsides, their bodies scratched by the thorns, their faces bruised by the rocks. Yet there was no one pursuing them!

9 When morning came, they began to clamber on hands and knees up the steep slopes as fast as they could. With difficulty they managed to escape into open country, where there was no impediment. Then they looked up and saw a large number of women walking along a path.

10 Taking those women for Barsauma's disciples, they were scared right out of their wits. So they retreated and went back down to the riverbank, getting tied up in knots on the steep slopes in their trepidation.

184. Cf. Mt 5:1f.

11 Now the bishop who was with them was an old man. Shaking and trembling with fear, he lamented his fate in the following words: "Woe to you, my white hairs! Woe to you, my darling eyes!"

12 They kept on the move, yet there was no one pursuing them. The curse which was written long ago in the Law had come true for them.

"If you doubt the Lord your God,[185]
you will totter and sway[186]
when confronted by 'a shaking leaf.'[187]

"'You will go out one way against your enemy and flee seven ways before him.'[188]

"You will shudder and 'you will flee, although there is no one pursuing you.'[189]

"Your enemy will be glad, because you scream and flee."

13 That is exactly what happened to those people who doubted the Lord Christ. They did not stop in their flight until they reached Samosata. There they found seven bishops holding a meeting about this business.

14 The bishop who was with those who had run away told his fellow bishops everything that had happened, ending with a warning: "Look out, Barsauma is on his way here to attack you!" Hearing this, those bishops left Samosata at once.

§ 149 The ninety-first sign. A chorepiscopus who threatens Barsauma is struck by the Lord and dies.

1 At Samosata there was a chorepiscopus, a proud and vainglorious man. Arrogance possessed him—it would be his downfall in the end. He spoke to those bishops in the hearing of all: "So are we all going to run away from one man and becoming the laughing stock of the land, because we are afraid of him? He has no more than thirty or forty disciples with him.

185. Cf. Dt 28:15.
186. Cf. Ps 62:3.
187. Lv 26:36.
188. Dt 28:25.
189. Lv 26:17.

2 "I am going to get a mob together, go out to meet Barsauma, and take him prisoner. I am going to put a collar around his throat and chains on the necks of his disciples and I am going to drag them all the way back here."

3 That very minute the scoundrel got up and drummed up everyone in the city. He sent for the brethren from the monasteries and the villagers. Bearing cudgels, clubs, and swords, this mob then marched against Barsauma.

4 As for him, he had not even considered going down to the city of Samosata against them, but had gone back to his beloved monastery, where he stayed for a few days.

5 While that chorepiscopus was on his way—he was marching across a broad plain, which was filled from edge to edge by the mob that he had mustered—about twenty of Barsauma's disciples went out to a certain mountain, from which they could watch that mob marching against them.

6 The bad chorepiscopus looked up and saw those brethren standing on the mountain opposite. In his eyes they appeared as a great army. "Who are those," he asked, "standing on the mountain?" Those who were marching with him answered: "Barsauma has sent messengers in all directions and brought together a great army to help him."

7 Hearing this, his heart shook, for all his insolence, and his bones knocked together. He nearly died of fear. He vomited, loosed his bowels, and was in mental torment.

8 "I implore you," he said, "take me back to the rear! My soul is in the throes of departure!" His underclothes were soiled, and his outer garment was filthy with the contents of his stomach.

9 They had to put him on a donkey to retreat. He got back to Samosata, but died after a long agony.

§ 150 *The ninety-second sign. A tribune offers to kill him.*

1 There was an Isaurian tribune, a professional soldier, with whom Barsauma's enemies exchanged oaths and drew up a legal contract. "If you use cunning to kill Barsauma," they promised, "each of us will give you one hundred darics. On top of that, we guarantee that you will receive ten darics from every bishop in the Roman Empire.

What is more, you will prove yourself a friend to the emperor and he will promote you."

2 The tribune accepted these conditions and swore to kill Barsauma. But when he went home and told his wife about it, she groaned. Trembling, she struck herself on the breast and on the face, then lifted up her voice and wept.

3 "Woe is me! Woe to my sons! Woe to the bones of my fathers in their graves!" She implored her husband with bitter tears not to do this thing, but he would not yield.

4 "As my Creator lives, who breathed life into me," said she at last, "if you do this deed, I am going to take my two infant sons and throw myself with them into the middle of the Euphrates. Not only the innocent Barsauma's blood, but mine and my sons', too, will be on your head on Judgment Day." Not even at this did he relent.

5 That night, in his sleep, he had the following vision. He was on his way to kill Barsauma. He looked up and saw him standing in a high and impregnable castle, clothed in garments whiter than snow and brighter than the sun. On his head was a crown, and his countenance was more dazzling than any lightning. Choirs of angels in white stood around him as ministers.

6 Barsauma challenged him: "Come, climb up to us, insolent and audacious man!" On the instant he fell from his horse, and the palm of his right hand was dislocated.

7 Barsauma challenged him again: "Get up! Come, climb up to us, importunate and wild-natured man!" Again he fell. This time his right foot was dislocated at the ankle.

8 Barsauma challenged him for the third time: "Get up, self-hater, and come to us!" He got up and climbed up to him, but Barsauma struck him with his hand on his cheek. "Get up and greet me! Be a peace-loving man, instead of an agent of aggression!"

9 At this point he awoke with a start. Immediately, he realized that his right wrist and his right ankle were dislocated and quivering. The thing he had seen in his sleep was waking reality. From the moment he awoke he was in excruciating pain.

10 He called his slaves. "Quick!" he said. "Tell Barsauma's enemies to come here!" "How have I ever injured you?" he protested, when they came. "Why should I die in agony, like this, because of you wicked apostates? Your denial of Christ has killed me!"

11 There and then he told them all what he had seen and showed them his painful dislocated joints. His wife was delighted; she stretched out her hands toward heaven and praised Christ.

12 "Go to Barsauma!" he implored her, with awe-inspiring oaths. "Fall down at his feet and beg him to heal my injuries!" She went gladly and journeyed on foot, now walking, now running, for about seventy-five miles,[190] day and night. When she reached Barsauma she fell down at his feet and wept convulsively. Then she told him everything that had happened.

13 He prayed, praised Christ, took oil, blessed it, and gave it to her. "Go home quickly," he said, "and anoint your husband with this oil! He will recover his health and live, in the name of our Lord Jesus Christ." She went home swiftly and anointed her husband with that oil. He was healed and lived to believe in Christ.

§ 151 The ninety-third sign. A bishop who threatens to kill him is struck by God and dies.

1 There was a bishop of Cyrrhus, to whom the emperor Marcian had subordinated all the bishops, giving him authority over all the East.[191] This man threatened to kill Barsauma and swore powerful oaths that he would not allow him to live.

2 He sent to the cities, inviting soldiers, wrote to the villages and monasteries, and mustered a great mob. He prepared an expedition to kill Barsauma and all his supporters. Many advised him to desist, but he swore that he would carry out his threat.

3 This rebel was on the point of setting out when the angel of the Lord struck him suddenly. He fell to the ground. The Lord had delivered him to an evil spirit, which tortured him. He proceeded to bite off his tongue and spit it out. His servants took him inside and hid him, ashamed to let this be seen. Tormented and disfigured by the devil, he died.

4 They intended to bury him in the martyrium of Saint Dionysius.[192] But while they were bearing the corpse in procession along the

190. 111 km.

191. Theodoret became bishop of Cyrrhus in 423; was exiled in 449 and reinstated in 451; and died in the 460s.

192. Cf. Theodoret, *Relig. hist.* 2.21.

street, Saint Dionysius appeared openly to the people, standing inside his chapel and shouting: "Do not bring that disfigured man in here! I will not have him buried with me!" There ensued a sudden general commotion; so they bore the damned man's corpse back along the street and buried him elsewhere.

§ 152 *The bishops write a letter about him to Marcian.*

1 When Barsauma's enemies saw him covered in glory, themselves in shame in every region, they realized they were no match for him. Then they assembled in number and took counsel how to get rid of him.

2 This assembly sent the following mendacious letter to the emperor: "From all the bishops and judges of the Roman Empire and from all Your Majesty's subjects to the glorious throne of your honor, respectful greetings!

3 "We write to inform Your powerful and zealous Majesty concerning the rebel Barsauma. This man is in rebellion against your fierce authority. He insults Your Majesty and exalts himself above Your Majesty's rule. Moreover, he blasphemes against Your Majesty's Faith and teaches paganism everywhere.

4 "Having mustered thousands of brigands and tens of thousands of bandits, he has subdued and occupied great swathes of land belonging to Your Majesty and there he withholds the corn supply from our lord, the emperor, and our lady, the empress.

5 "He has driven bishops from their churches and forced judges to leave their cities. He has dismissed the original priests from their altars of sacrifice and appointed other priests, although he is no bishop.

6 "He has collected much gold and filled great treasuries. Unless Your Majesty takes action, he is going to subjugate many regions.

7 "We therefore petition Your Majesty's fearsome authority to adopt the same zeal as your servants and send a great force of soldiers against him. Let the great force he has mustered be destroyed and let the rebel himself be killed!"

8 When Marcian received this letter full of lies, he was angered and disturbed. He sent an open letter (σάκρα) to the great cities and dispatched a great force of soldiers to arrest Barsauma and bring him

to the capital. All this came to Barsauma's ears. He was delighted to hear of it and gave thanks to Christ.

§ 153 *He curses the emperor Marcian.*

1 Exultant, he made a solemn statement: "I have an unshakable faith in Christ that Marcian's authority will never be imposed on me. He will not see my face in this world, nor I his hateful visage. I place my hope in the victorious Crucified, whom I, at least, have not denied, that my death is going to rid this world of Marcian."

2 After this, he was moved to climb up to his monastery. Five miles[193] away from his monastery, he stopped to spend the night somewhere.

3 While his companions ate supper, one of his disciples felt compelled by God to make an announcement in front of Barsauma and in the hearing of all: "Our master is soon to be taken away from us. Of this you may be sure!" This was a prophetic inspiration.

§ 154 *He has a vision concerning his illness.*

1 The following morning, before daybreak, Barsauma climbed up to his cave. A great multitude from all countries was assembled to see him. He continued to live for about two weeks in his monastery.

2 One morning, Barsauma spoke openly in front of his disciples: "Last night I saw the angel of the Lord. He stood there in front of me and said: 'Barsauma, I am here to give you advance intelligence of what is going to happen. You are going to fall ill; and that illness is going to be worse than any you have had.'"

3 He had hardly finished speaking when his soul grew heavy and he fell ill. So began the grievous illness by which he would depart from this world.

4 He summoned one of his disciples, a man filled with zeal for the Faith and rich in wisdom and eloquence, and said to him: "Come, my son! Let me send you into Persia! Go also to Armenia! Visit the bishops of those countries and persuade them to defend the Faith!

5 "Today, in case I die before you return, I am going to give you the blessing which fathers and masters ought to give their sons at their

193. 7.5 km.

death; and you, likewise, are going to pray for me, as disciples and sons are obliged to pray for their fathers!"

6 He spoke with him on many subjects, then gave him his blessing and dismissed him. At peace, that disciple set off for Persia.

§ 155 *The ninety-fourth sign. A great earthquake occurs before his death.*

1 A few days later the time came for the champion (ἀθλητής) to be crowned. Before he died, God gave a terrible sign of the pain of that parting.

2 A great earthquake occurred in the country where he dwelt, and the catastrophe made itself felt in all the surrounding region. The foundations of the earth shook. Mountains quaked, hills shuddered, crags crumbled. Buildings tottered, corbels fell off, upper stories collapsed. Palaces were knocked down, villages ruined, their owners buried. The earth groaned, the hills complained, and a mournful noise between a roar and a moan could be heard from the belly of the earth and from the very foundations of the mountains.

3 The earth continually groaned and tottered in this way for several days before his death; and the groaning lingered in that region for six months after his death. Only then did the earth's din fall still, as though bringing closure to a period of mourning.

4 Just as the children of Israel performed a ritual of mourning after the death of the zealous Josiah,[194] so the Northern Region made lamentation on a vast scale for the death of Barsauma. It was not only people that grieved; the earth herself was in mourning. Even before human beings articulated their grief, the mountains and the hills were grieving.

§ 156 *The ninety-fifth sign. An angel speaks with him and tells him about his coming death.*

1 That night the angel of the Lord appeared to him: "Barsauma, what I am going to tell you is the truth: four days from now our Lord Jesus Christ is going to send me to bring you to Him. Give instructions concerning your monastery and all your desires!"[195]

194. 2 Kgs 23:30; cf. 2 Kgs 23:1–25.
195. Cf. Mt 1:20; 2:13, 19.

§ 157 *His death.*

1 The following morning, Barsauma summoned the brethren who lived with him and told them what the angel had said. They began to weep and to mourn, but Barsauma said: "Whether you like it or not, I am going to leave you."

2 Then he began to speak astonishing words which came straight from God. Day and night, four days long, he gave instructions. Then he blessed everyone by rank, according to precedence.

3 Afterward he lay down on a bed and said: "Farewell! Pray for me!" He crossed himself, praised Christ, and gave up his spirit to God. So he fell peacefully asleep and rested from his labor.

4 Barsauma departed from this world on the first of February and was buried on the third.

§ 158 *The ninety-sixth sign. A pillar of fire appears when he yields his spirit to Christ.*

1 Now the time when he gave up his spirit to Christ was about the fourth hour of the night. At that very hour, a certain priest, who happened to be standing with a number of people some way off and looking that way, saw a bright light flashing from heaven and a pillar of fire descending to earth and alighting on Barsauma's head.

2 Others also, who were further away from there, saw the pillar of fire at that hour. As for that priest who was standing and watching, he discerned the truth and announced to those who were with him: "At this very hour, Barsauma's spirit is ascending to heaven."

3 An old man, near the end of his life, looked out at that same moment and saw from afar that pillar of fire. He was one of the righteous, who dwelt in another country, six days' journey from Barsauma's monastery. Having the gift of discernment, he, too, understood.

4 That pillar of fire remained above the monastery of Barsauma for a long time, then it was observed to recede into heaven. Barsauma's spirit was taken up into heaven in the column of fire.

5 This miracle resembles that of the prophet Elijah.

A chariot of fire carried the body of the zealous and holy Elijah up to heaven.[196]

196. 2 Kgs 2:11–13.

The column of fire carried the spirit of the zealous and holy Barsauma up to heaven.

Elijah's body was taken up, and his mantle was left among men as a blessing.

Barsauma's spirit went up, and his body remained with us as a blessing.

6 As for the emperor Marcian, as soon as he heard of Barsauma's death, he canceled the military expedition against him.

§ 159 *The ninety-seventh sign. The emperor Marcian dies.*

1 Now because it was appropriate that this other thing should also happen and that the words spoken by Barsauma before he fell ill should come true—namely, "I hope, by the Crucified, whom I, at least, have not denied, that Marcian is never going to impose his authority on me. He will not see my face, nor I his hateful visage"—everything turned out just as he had requested.

2 Moreover, it was necessary that what Barsauma had said before his death should also be fulfilled—namely, "As Christ is true to me, my death will get rid of Marcian."

3 For this reason the disciple who had been sent by Barsauma to Persia and Armenia when he fell ill, departed from Armenia and arrived in Syria at the time of the harvest. He went in and prayed in the place where Barsauma was buried and wept great tears there.

4 Then he left Barsauma's monastery and set off on a journey. He went to the city of Hemesa (Ḥimṣ),[197] which is opposite Mount Lebanon, and entered the place where the head of John the Baptist is entombed to pray.

5 The door of the niche where Saint John's head was kept was secured with iron locks; but when that disciple reached the door, it opened for him by God's will. The disciple went in and put his face in front of John the Baptist's head and wept tears of sorrow there.

6 Then he took a sheet of papyrus and a pot of ink and went and sat apart on his own. He wept into the pot and so mixed the ink with

197. Barrington Atlas 68, C4.

his tears. He took up a reed-pen and wrote the following on the sheet of papyrus.

7 "From so-and-so, a distressed, persecuted, exiled man, to you, my lord John, head of those who live in the wilderness, greeting!

8 "My lord, I hereby accuse Marcian, my own persecutor, of confusing the true Way and of abandoning his faith in God. My lord, by the senior authority which you possess, please urge Christ, who loves you—you have been called 'the Friend of the Bridegroom'[198]—to have Marcian's authority taken away and given to another!"

9 He wrote these words and many more on the sheet of papyrus. Included in the scroll was the name of Proterius, who had become bishop of Alexandria the Great, because at that time he was killing those who would not deny Christ, for he had killed more than thirty thousand Christians, both men and women.

10 Also included were the names of other wicked people. At the end of the scroll he wrote: "My lord, I do not address my accusation to a dead man, nor do I apply for judgment to a skeleton or a corpse. I address my accusation to a man who is alive in Christ, and in whom dwells the life-giving Spirit of Holiness."

§ 160 Saint John appears and speaks of Marcian's death.

1 When the document had been concluded and sealed, the man who had written it took it and laid it on Saint John's head. Then he spent the night in that chapel. Many were sleeping there. Around midnight something like a man appeared to many, standing in the middle of the chapel and proclaiming at the top of its voice: "The emperor Marcian is dead, because a Christian has brought an accusation against him."

2 So again there appeared (something) in the likeness of another man, who was holding that scroll and reading; and he was uttering death-threats against Marcian, because he saw the disciple of Barsauma, who had written that letter.[199]

198. Jn 3:29.

199. This section contradicts § 160.1, which says Marcian is already dead.

§ 161 *The disciple who wrote the note to the holy John has a vision.*

1 Saint John appeared as though dressed in clothes as white as the sun. He came and stood next to the man who had written the scroll, and revealed to him many things which were about to happen.

2 "Do not be distressed, or weep," he told him, "but go to the place which I am going to tell you about. You will see, some people will come to that place and tell you about everything you wrote to me and give you the good news about the death of Marcian and about the burning of Proterius of Alexandria; and again, they will tell you of the others about whom you wrote to me."

3 Then that disciple departed from the city of Hemesa and went to the place he had been told about; and while he was standing there in prayer, behold, some people came up to him and told him the good news about the death of Marcian;[200] and they told him how Proterius had been burned in Alexandria the Great;[201] and they told him what had happened to those others whose names were written in the scroll.

4 Now these things truly happened in this way; and if there is anyone who is unwilling to accept them, he will have to answer for the blasphemy of his tongue!

§ 162 *The ninety-eighth sign.*

1 Now it happened after this that a fatal contagion broke out in a certain country. The inhabitants of that country came and took the oil of prayer and the holy dust and oil from where Barsauma's body was buried; and at the same time the contagion ceased to spread.

§ 163 *The ninety-ninth sign.*

1 There was a well-known man in a certain city, who had been tormented by Satan for a long time. The man who was subject to this tribulation was of the same persuasion as the persecutors of Barsauma.

2 This man had a vision that he should go and pray beside Barsauma's bones. He did so and was cured. Then the persecutors of Bar-

200. Marcian died in January 457.

201. Proterius was patriarch of Alexandria from 451 to 457. On his death, see Evagrius, *Eccl. hist.* 2.8.

sauma were put to shame and began, one by one, to repent inwardly. Many of them went to that place, weeping and distressed.

3 Many signs are performed today on Barsauma's bones, and many sick people go to his resting place and are healed. Devils and evil spirits are cruelly tormented in his presence.

§ 164 [*The First Colophon*]

1 As for my incapable and insignificant person, the Lord knows my name. May he pardon my sins! At a time when I was tried in many ways, I was compelled by overwhelming love to compose a memoir of the above events. But lest my narrative become burdensome to the audience by its length, I also left many other signs unwritten. Moreover, what I have written is known not only to me but also to many others.

2 Whoever reads and believes, whoever hears and affirms, and whoever praises Christ for what he hears shall have a share in the exertions of Barsauma and a part, together with all those who are chosen, in the covenant of the righteous!

3 Whoever prays for me when he hears what I have written shall not pray to God in vain when he asks forgiveness for his sins! Whoever remembers me with affection when these words are read out loud shall be remembered by our Lord Jesus Christ on the day of his Second Coming[202] and receive new life together with the upright and the righteous, now and always, forever and ever, Amen!

§ 165 [*The Second Colophon*]

1 Now it was the priest Samuel who wrote down these acts (consisting) of the achievements of the champion (ἀθλητής) Barsauma. He was one of Barsauma's first disciples. But all of us know that all these things have been written down in truth.

2 This same priest Samuel also wrote many metrical homilies (*mīmrē*) and teaching-songs (*madrošē*) and sermons (*tūrgomē*) on the Faith and on various subjects; and refutations of all superstitions (*deḥloto*); and a refutation of the Dyophysites; and fine commentaries on the Scriptures.

3 As for us, slaves of Christ, who have concluded this book, we conjure you by almighty God, let no one dare to change even one of its

202. Cf. Mt 24f.

excellent words! Whoever copies from this manuscript shall copy them out right down to this point!

4 May the grace of our Lord and His mercy be on all of us, now and always, forever and ever, Amen!

[Subscription in the oldest manuscript, of 1085]

§ 166 End of the story of Barsauma, the Head of the Mourners in the Northern Massif in the region (κλίμα) of Syria. May his prayers be with us! Amen!

Founded in 1893,
UNIVERSITY OF CALIFORNIA PRESS
publishes bold, progressive books and journals on topics in the arts, humanities, social sciences, and natural sciences—with a focus on social justice issues—that inspire thought and action among readers worldwide.

The UC PRESS FOUNDATION
raises funds to uphold the press's vital role as an independent, nonprofit publisher, and receives philanthropic support from a wide range of individuals and institutions—and from committed readers like you. To learn more, visit ucpress.edu/supportus.